Bluegrass Gospel Jams

By

Ron Camerrer

Ron Camerrer
Fort Collins, Colorado
www.bluegrassgospeljam.com

© 2012 Ron Camerrer. All rights reserved.

No part of this book may be reproduced, stored in a retrieval system, or transmitted by any means without the written permission of the author.

First published by Ron Camerrer 06/1/2012

ISBN: 978-0615647371

Printed in the United States of America

Bible Verses: New International Version (NIV) translation

Dedication

This book is dedicated to all the musicians, audiences, and participants who have, over all the years, supported the faith concepts of the Bluegrass Gospel Jams. We believe that God's word gets spread through participation.

Special thanks go to Ken Hoornbeek and Nathan Weinland for all their encouragement and input over the years.

By identifying motivational gifts, Ken Hoornbeek has a passion for helping people find their *"life purpose and calling."* Find your passion and choose wisely for a career or college major.

Ken also helps authors who have passion, publish their works. Thanks, Ken, for helping me with this book.

Ron Camerrer

Core Bible Verses

Ephesians 5: 19

Speak to one another with psalms, hymns and spiritual songs. Sing and make music in your heart to the Lord, always giving thanks to God the Father for everything, in the name of our Lord Jesus Christ.

Hebrews 13 1-2

Keep on loving each others as brothers. Do not forget to entertain strangers, for by so doing, some people have entertained angels without knowing it.

Table of Contents

Prelude 4

Chapter 1 - What is a Bluegrass Gospel Jam? 7

Chapter 2 - History of Bluegrass Music 12

Chapter 3 - Bluegrass Gospel Jam Culture Defined 22

Chapter 4 - Two Kinds Of Jams 25

Chapter 5 - Be A Bluegrass Gospel Jam Musician 35

Chapter 6 - Starting A Bluegrass Gospel Jam 43

Chapter 7 - Leading A Bluegrass Gospel Jam 57

Chapter 8 - Grow A Bluegrass Gospel Jam 77

Chapter 9 - Cultivate An Outreach 79

Chapter 10 - Wisdom Insights 92

Chapter 11 - Maintaining The Momentum 108

Chapter 12 - Seven Essential Principles 125

Chapter 13 - "Tidbits Of Faith To Chew On" 138

Chapter 14 - My Bluegrass Gospel Jam Journey 166

Prelude

First In Line

I sat there in a chair with my guitar, my eyes surveying the other musicians playing in the Bluegrass Gospel Jam. This was the first Jam of the year, in January. Only last week, I had gone to the Urgent Care facility. Within eight minutes after arrival, I was rolled onto a bed and into an ambulance to be transported to the emergency room of the main hospital downtown.

Earlier, I emailed my daughter in nearby Windsor, Colorado. I asked her if she would come and take me to the Urgent Care Center. I told her in my email, *"I was having a lot of trouble breathing."* When we arrived, there were two lines of people, waiting to check in. A nurse came over and asked me some quick questions. I was immediately seated in a wheelchair and, like a burst of wind, whisked past all the people standing in line. Within a small sheet-shrouded room, I felt like an actor in a *"day-time soap-opera hospital scene."* Everyone was rushing around, asking me questions, poking me with needles, moving technical machines around, with everyone talking simultaneously, to me, and to each other. My bed seemed like the interior of a hornet's nest.

"You are going to be all right, Dad. They are going to be taking good care of you. You are going to get good care."

Two different times, I felt a tear running down from my eyes. My voice wavered. I was genuinely scared from all the attention I was receiving. The next thing I knew, I was staring up at the top of an ambulance roof that had a small flat cylinder that looked like a smoke detector. I was praying upwards towards God and beyond that smoke detector. No siren was wailing. I felt every bump and rattle in that ambulance. My weak heart had deposited fluid in my lungs.

After spending almost a whole day on oxygen in the hospital emergency room, I was sent home with a cylinder of oxygen and a white plastic tube for my head and nose. I spent an entire week at my daughter's house, on oxygen, resting and eating right. I lost eleven pounds. After that week, when I returned home...I stayed on oxygen and had lunch delivered from Meals On Wheels. As I recuperated, I had to take my car in for repairs. Without transportation, I was entirely homebound for two more days. During that time, I took a surefire look at this most recent wake-up call.

Now, two weeks later, sitting in that chair on the stage, I observed the emerging assembly of participants in the *"Bluegrass Gospel Jam."* I pleasantly pondered the outcomes that I helped create. The Jam is a place for emerging and blossoming talents. It's an outlet for encouraging participation. The Jam is a place where fun time is inspired.

Raymond & his wife, Eva, had driven all the way from Fort Morgan, about two hours away. This was their first Jam. Vicki, Mo, and Mo's granddaughter, Brooke, arrived. Jim and his daughter, Cindy, were there. I hadn't seen Jim for a long time. He had an oxygen cylinder at his side with a tube running up to his nose. Soon, at my encouragement, Jim was up front with his electric bass, playing and singing along. Soon, I had Eva up front singing with Raymond and the trio of girls. Soon, I also joined the singing group of girls. We developed an impromptu five-person choir. As the Jam progressed, I looked around again at all the comings and goings around me.

I noticed that Jim's plastic oxygen tube had been taken away from his face. His oxygen cylinder was on the floor behind him. Jim was taking turns choosing songs and singing into a microphone. In previous Jams, I had never heard Jim sing. To my right, Steve came in. He was a classical pianist. Now he was playing a guitar that he had purchased and had begun practicing just a year ago. I also heard Steve singing for the first time. I moved the microphone over to Steve during his song. As I listened and participated in the ambiance of the developing music, I was aware of God's awesome presence within the Jam. We sang versions of *"Mansion Over The Hilltop"* three times in a row. I was reminded in my spirit, *"The Jam is good. Keep on doing it."*

Even in my weakened health condition, I realized that the Jam was accomplishing God's purposes. I comprehended that I was the energizing catalyst for the evolving camaraderie of genuine, wholesome, long-lasting fun time, *"within a gospel atmosphere."* I reminded myself that I had helped plan it this way. I understood that I was God's chosen instrument to carry out this task. I was receiving God's encouragement as I encouraged others to join in.

By desire and example, the Bluegrass Gospel Jams continue to grow. *"Mustard Seeds of Bluegrass Gospel Songs"* continue to sprout. Opportunities abound because we step out and share gospel songs. Someone said, *"A bluegrass song is three chords and a poem."*

"A bluegrass gospel song is three chords and part of a bible verse."

I'm eternally happy that I get to be involved. Bluegrass Gospel Jams have turned into a viable ministry, reaching people in ways I never could have done on my own. I give full credit to God for what he is doing through me. You can have that same opportunity. Continue to read this book with anticipation. The Bluegrass Gospel Jams are an ongoing achievement pursuit, reaching others with the gospel through music and songs... a ministry *"Without Walls."*

Chapter 1 - What is a Bluegrass Gospel Jam?

It all begins when a small group of musicians gather together to play bluegrass music. Typically the musicians gather in a circle and take turns choosing songs. This circle gathering is called a *"jam."* As backup, the other musicians play along. Each player then takes his or her respective turn choosing a song. Usually the jam is an informal open forum, where all skill levels are encouraged. Playing together as a group accelerates learning and enjoyment. Some jams are entirely acoustical (stringed instruments only.) Some jams are a combination of acoustical and amplified instruments. The Bluegrass Gospel Jams encourage *"unseen talents"* to emerge. We practice creativity. I feel a Bluegrass Gospel Jam sets the stage for practicing *"Peace."*

A Bluegrass Gospel Jam is also the catalyst for creating and building a legacy for future and current generations. By sponsoring and promoting the formation of new bluegrass gospel jams, we have found a need. We are fulfilling that need. Have you ever pondered that thought about music? The magic of music helps you find that connection within your soul. Have you tried to find the music inside your soul? A bluegrass gospel jam can lead the way.

Can you, or someone you encourage, learn to play an instrument? Can you, or someone you encourage, learn to sing? Yes, it's happening for me. Everything comes from asking folks to participate. If we make a mistake in a Jam, we just keep on going. When we continually interact with other people by inviting folks to participate, amazingly good harmonious sounds burst forth. You are invited!

Who Attends?

Anyone who has *"a song in their heart and a tap in their toe"* will attend. Bluegrass Gospel Jams spread primarily by word-of-mouth announcements. We welcome all skills and anyone who wants to come and listen. Friends of friends come all the time. I carry invitation cards with me at all times. I pass them out whenever someone inquires about my Bluegrass Gospel Jam logo jacket. I pass the cards out at every jam. I give several invitation cards to each musician so that they can also become *"Jam Ambassadors."*

Colossians 3: 17

And whatever you do, whether in word or deed, do it all in the name of the Lord Jesus, giving thanks to God the Father through him.

If you choose, you can make a Bluegrass Gospel Jam happen. You may or may not be a musician. You may or may not be a proficient *"A-1"* skilled singer or instrument performer. It doesn't matter. If your goal is to reach others with the gospel message, you can achieve that worthwhile goal through your participating in gospel music environments that *you help create.*

By faith, God will send you the people you need to start the ball rolling and to carry on. A jam is definitely a joint team effort. A God-guided faith team produces miraculous outcomes.

Psalm 23: 1-3

The Lord is my shepherd; I shall not be in want. He makes me lie down in green pastures, he leads me beside quiet waters, he restores my soul.

Over time, and through experience, I have learned what works and doesn't work. I am still in the continual learning process. In this guide, I have outlined many obstacles a leader will probably encounter. I have included solutions for you to keep in mind. Hopefully you will find even better solutions than I have. In fact, I encourage you to send your victory and triumph stories to me. My desire is to *encourage you to encourage others.*

You will continually encounter new challenges simply because you are working with people. Volunteer musicians are a very special type of challenge. Musicians are creative artists. Your job as a leader is to help develop wholesome musical and camaraderie relationships. Your job is to seek and find folks who share your vision of spreading the gospel. It is wise to concentrate upon all the victories you experience. I have discovered that victories predominately outnumber the obstacles, ninety-eight percent to two-percent.

Love The People

This is the key component to holding successful jams. How will they know we are Christians? *"By our love for one another."* Demonstration and action are more powerful than words. People tend to return to an environment where they are continually learning. Sharing music creates a bond of friendship that glues people's lives together.

Guidance And Motivation

"Your own basic attitude of mind" is the one primary principle that will determine the outcome of your jams. Your underlying goals can be similar to mine, but you cannot become, *"Ron."* I couldn't possibly become, *"you."* Each new jam will be different. The principles remain the same. If you do not have some definite underlying and pure motivating purpose, your jam can dissipate quickly, and soon fade away.

I had to learn *"guidance"* through *"on-the-job"* experience. When you have a basic goal of sharing your faith, changing and adjusting are easy to do. When you are motivated by doing something you really enjoy, the effort, long work, and planning are worth it all. Make sure you plan to have fun. *Bluegrass Gospel Jams are designed to be fun.*

The course corrections I have made all along the way have extended the longevity and effectiveness of the jams. I encourage you to be prepared and ready for the good results that start coming in regularly. Even though various difficulties sometimes appear, rise above them and handle with prayer. Stumbling blocks offer opportunities to excel. There will be more about this concept later.

Biblical Description Of A Bluegrass Gospel Jam

Romans 12: 9-13

"Love must be sincere. Hate what is evil; cling to what is good. Be devoted to one another in brotherly love. Honor one another above yourselves. Never be lacking in Zeal, but keep your spiritual fervor, serving the Lord. Be joyful in hope, patient in affliction, faithful in prayer. Share with God's people who are in need. Practice hospitality."

By the way, Satan doesn't like what you and I are doing. Be prepared for the hidden attacks and problems that the devil sends. He will test you at your weakest personality points. He wants you to fail. Please remember that God wants you to succeed.

Proverbs 16: 3

Commit to the Lord whatever you do, and your plans will succeed.

Chapter 2 - History of Bluegrass Music

In the 1930s, in Chicago, Thomas A. Dorsey (best known as author of the song, "Precious Lord, Take My Hand"), who had spent the 1920s writing secular music, turned full time to gospel music, established a publishing house, and invented the black gospel style of piano music. He had many trials in his life that he overcame concerning his health and his wife died. He dedicated all of his musical talent to the service of the LORD. Thomas gained knowledge of his religion from his father who was a Baptist minister and took up on piano from his mother who was his teacher. He started working with black blues pianists when they moved to Atlanta. It has been said that 1930 was the year when modern gospel music began, because the National Baptist Convention first publicly endorsed the music at its 1930 meeting. Dorsey was responsible for developing the musical careers of many African-American artists, such as Mahalia Jackson. One of the favorite bluegrass gospel song classics is in fact, Dorsey's "Precious Lord, Take my Hand."

We play Dorsey's song consistently in our current bluegrass gospel jam... in bluegrass style...

Radio continued to develop an audience for gospel music, a fact that was commemorated in Albert E. Brumley's 1937 song, "Turn Your Radio On" (which is still being published in gospel song books). In 1972, a recording of "Turn Your Radio On" by the Lewis Family was nominated for "Gospel Song of the Year" in the Gospel Music Association's Dove Awards.

The various types of music brought with the people who began migrating to America in the early 1600s are considered to be the roots of bluegrass music---including dance music and ballads from Ireland, Scotland and England, as well as African American gospel music and blues. (In fact, slaves from Africa brought the design idea for the banjo--an instrument now integral to the bluegrass sound.)

As the early Jamestown settlers began to spread out into the Carolinas, Tennessee, Kentucky and the Virginias, they composed new songs about day-to-day life experiences in the new land. Since most of these people lived in rural areas, the songs reflected life on the farm or in the hills and this type of music was called "mountain music" or "country music." The invention of the phonograph and the onset of the radio in the early 1900s brought this old-time music out of the rural Southern mountains to people all over the United States.

Good singing became a more important part of country music. Singing stars like Jimmie Rodgers, family bands like the Carter family from Virginia and duet teams like the Monroe Brothers from Kentucky contributed greatly to the advancement of traditional country music.

The Monroe Brothers were one of the most popular duet teams of the 1920s and into the 1930s. Charlie played the guitar, Bill played the mandolin and they sang duets in harmony. When the brothers split up as a team in 1938, both went on to form their own bands. Since Bill was a native of Kentucky, the Bluegrass State, he decided to call his band "Bill Monroe and the Blue Grass Boys," and this band's sound birthed a new form of country music.

"Bill Monroe and the Blue Grass Boys" first appeared on the Grand Ole Opry in 1939 and soon became one of the most popular touring bands out of Nashville's WSM studios. Bill's new band was different from other traditional country music bands of the time because of its hard driving and powerful sound, utilizing traditional acoustic instruments and featuring highly distinctive vocal harmonies. This music incorporated songs and rhythms from string band, gospel (black and white), work songs and "shouts" of black laborers, country and blues music repertoires. Vocal selections included duet, trio and quartet harmony singing in addition to Bill's powerful "high lonesome" solo lead singing. After experimenting with various instrumental combinations, Bill settled on mandolin, banjo, fiddle, guitar and bass as the format for his band. The guitar originally came from Spain. The mandolin, as well as the fiddle and acoustic bass (both from the violin family), originally came from Italy.

While many fans of bluegrass music date the genre back to 1939, when Monroe formed his first Blue Grass Boys band, most believe that the classic bluegrass sound jelled in 1945, shortly after Earl Scruggs, a 21 year old banjo player from North Carolina, joined the band. Scruggs played an innovative three-finger picking style on the banjo that energized enthusiastic audiences, and has since come to be called simply, "Scruggs style" banjo. Equally influential in the classic 1945 line-up of the Blue Grass Boys were Lester Flatt, from Sparta, Tenn. on guitar and lead vocals against Monroe's tenor; Chubby Wise, from Florida, on fiddle; and Howard Watts, also known by his comedian name, "Cedric Rainwater," on acoustic bass.

When first Earl Scruggs, and then Lester Flatt left, Monroe's band eventually formed their own group known as The Foggy Mountain Boys. They decided to include the resophonic guitar, or Dobro, into their band format. The Dobro is often included in bluegrass band formats today as a result. Burkett H. "Uncle Josh" Graves, from Tellico Plains, Tenn., heard Scruggs' three-finger style of picking in 1949 and adapted it to the then, almost obscure slide bar instrument. With Flatt & Scruggs from 1955-1969, Graves introduced his widely emulated, driving, bluesy style on the Dobro. The Dopyera Brothers, immigrant musicians/inventors, invented the Dobro in the United States originally from the Slovak Republic. The brand name, "Dobro," comes from DOpyera BROthers.

From 1948-1969, Flatt & Scruggs were a major force in introducing bluegrass music to America through national television, at major universities and coliseums, and at schoolhouse appearances in numerous towns. Scruggs wrote and recorded one of bluegrass music's most famous instrumentals, "Foggy Mountain Breakdown," which was used in the soundtrack for the film, *Bonnie & Clyde*. In 1969 he established an innovative solo career with his three sons as "The Earl Scruggs Revue." Scruggs still records and performs selected dates in groups that usually include his sons, Randy on guitar and Gary on bass.

After parting with Scruggs in 1969, Lester Flatt continued successfully with his own group, "The Nashville Grass," performing steadily until shortly before his death in 1979.

By the 1950s, people began referring to this style of music as "bluegrass music." Bluegrass bands began forming all over the country and Bill Monroe became the acknowledged "Father of Bluegrass Music."

In the 1960s, the concept of the "bluegrass festival" was first introduced, featuring bands that had seemed to be in competition with each other for a relatively limited audience on the same bill at weekend festivals across the country. Carlton Haney, from Reidsville, N.C., is credited with envisioning and producing the first weekend-long bluegrass music festival, held at Fincastle, Va. in 1965.

The increased availability of traditional music recordings, nationwide indoor and outdoor bluegrass festivals and movie, television and commercial soundtracks featuring bluegrass music have aided in bringing this music out of modern day obscurity. Lester Flatt and Earl Scruggs & the Foggy Mountain Boys achieved national prominence with tour sponsorship by Martha White Flour and for playing the soundtrack for the previously mentioned film, *Bonnie and Clyde*, as well as on a television show called, *The Beverly*

Hillbillies. The *Deliverance* movie soundtrack also featured bluegrass music-in particular, *"Dueling Banjos,"* performed by Eric Weissberg on banjo and Steve Mandel on guitar. In 2001, the triple platinum selling soundtrack for the Coen Brothers movie, "*O Brother, Where Art Thou?*" attracted wider audiences for bluegrass and traditional country music.

Bill Monroe passed away on September 9, 1996, four days before his 85th birthday. In May 1997, Bill Monroe was inducted into the Rock and Roll Hall of Fame because of the profound influence of his music on the popular music of this country. He is also a member of the Country Music Hall of Fame and the Bluegrass Music Hall of Honor.

Bluegrass music is now performed and enjoyed around the world. In addition to the to the classic style born in 1945 that is still performed widely, bluegrass bands today reflect influences from a variety of sources including traditional and fusion jazz, contemporary country music, Celtic music, rock & roll ("newgrass" or progressive bluegrass), old--time music and Southern gospel music--in addition to lyrics translated to various languages.

Thanks to IBMA *for contributing the above synopsis. To visit the IBMA website, click on* IBMA FanFest: Nashville TN

The music now known as bluegrass was frequently used to accompany a rural dancing style known as buckdancing, flatfooting or clogging. As the bluegrass sound spread to urban areas, listening to it for its own sake increased, especially after the advent of audio recording. In 1948, bluegrass emerged as a genre within the post-war country-music industry, a period of time characterized as the golden era or wellspring of "traditional bluegrass." From its earliest days, bluegrass has been recorded and performed by professional musicians. Although amateur bluegrass musicians and trends such as "parking-lot picking" are too important to be ignored, it is professional musicians who have set the direction of the style.

The topical and narrative themes of many bluegrass songs are highly reminiscent of folk music. In fact, many songs that are widely considered to be bluegrass are in reality older works that are performed in the bluegrass style. Hence the interplay between bluegrass and folk forms has been academically studied. Folklorist Dr. Neil Rosenberg, for example, shows that most devoted bluegrass fans and musicians are familiar with traditional folk songs and old-time music, and that these songs are often played at shows, festivals and jams.

Monroe's 1946 to 1948 band, which featured banjo prodigy Earl Scruggs, singer-guitarist Lester Flatt, fiddler Chubby Wise and bassist Howard Watts (also known as "Cedric Rainwater")—sometimes called "the original bluegrass band"—created the definitive sound and instrumental configuration that remains a model to this day. By some arguments, while the Blue Grass Boys were the only band playing this music, it was just their unique sound; it could not be considered a musical style until other bands began performing in similar fashion. In 1948, the Stanley Brothers recorded the traditional song "Molly and Tenbrooks" in the Blue Grass Boys' style, arguably the point in time that bluegrass emerged as a distinct musical form. As Ralph Stanley himself said about the origins of the genre and its name at the Granada Theater in Dallas:

"Oh, (Monroe) was the first. But it wasn't called bluegrass back then. It was just called "old time mountain *hillbilly* music." When they started doing the bluegrass festivals in 1965, everybody got together and wanted to know what to call the show, y'know. It was decided that since Bill was the oldest man, and was from the Bluegrass state of *Kentucky* and he had the Blue Grass Boys, it would be called 'bluegrass.'"

Third generation Bluegrass developed in the mid-1980s. Bluegrass grew, matured and broadened from the music played in previous years. This generation redefined "mainstream bluegrass." High-quality sound equipment allowed each band member to be miked independently, exemplified by Tony Rice Unit and The Bluegrass Album Band. Tony Rice showcased elaborate lead guitar solos, and other bands followed. The electric bass became a general, but not universal, alternative to the traditional acoustic bass, though electrification of other instruments continued to meet resistance outside progressive circles. Nontraditional chord progressions also became more widely accepted. On the other hand, this generation saw a renaissance of more traditional songs, played in the newer style. The **Johnson Mountain Boys** were one of the decade's most popular touring groups, and played strictly **traditional bluegrass**.

In recent decades Bluegrass music has reached a broader audience. Major mainstream country music performers have recorded bluegrass albums, including Dolly Parton and Patty Loveless, who each released several bluegrass albums. Since the late 1990s, Ricky Skaggs, who began as a bluegrass musician and crossed over to mainstream country in the 1980s, returned to bluegrass with his band Kentucky Thunder. The Coen Brothers' released the movie *O Brother, Where Art Thou?* in (2000), with an old-time and bluegrass soundtrack, and the *Down from the Mountain* music tour and documentary resulting.

Meanwhile, festivals like the Telluride Bluegrass Festival, Rocky-Grass in Lyons, Colorado and the Nederland, Colorado based Yonder Mountain String Band in the United States, and Druhá Tráva in the Czech Republic attract large audiences while expanding the range of progressive bluegrass in the college-jam band atmospheres, often called "jamgrass." Bluegrass fused with jazz in the music of Bela Fleck and The Flecktones, Tony Rice, Sam Bush, Doc Watson, and others.

Instrumentation

Bluegrass is traditionally played on acoustic stringed instruments. The fiddle, five-string banjo, guitar, mandolin, and upright bass (string bass) are often joined by the resonator guitar (also referred to as a Dobro) and (occasionally) harmonica. This instrumentation originated in rural dance bands and is the basis on which the earliest bluegrass bands were formed. Often, a washtub base, spoons, and old time washboard scrubbers are employed for rhythm. Autoharps and Q-Chords are now emerging. Bluegrass gospel music has a continually developing style of its own. The guitar is now most commonly played with a style referred to as flat picking, unlike the style of seminal bluegrass guitarist Lester Flatt, who used a thumb and finger pick. Banjo players often use the three-finger picking style made popular by Earl Scruggs. Fiddlers will frequently play in thirds and fifths, producing a sound that is characteristic to the bluegrass style.

In regular bluegrass, one or more instruments each takes its turn playing the melody and improvising around it, while the others perform accompaniment; this is especially typified in tunes called breakdowns. This is in contrast to old-time music, in which all instruments play the melody together or one instrument carries the lead throughout while the others provide accompaniment. Breakdowns are often characterized by rapid tempos and unusual instrumental dexterity and sometimes by complex chord changes. Bluegrass music has attracted a diverse and loyal following worldwide. Bluegrass pioneer Bill Monroe characterized the genre as: "Scottish bagpipes and ole-time fiddlin'. It has a high lonesome sound."

Instrumentation has been an ongoing topic of debate. Traditional bluegrass performers believe the "correct" instrumentation is that used by Bill Monroe's band, the Blue Grass Boys (mandolin, played by Monroe, fiddle, guitar, banjo and bass). Departures from the traditional instrumentation have included accordion, harmonica, piano, autoharp, drums, electric guitar, and electric versions of other common bluegrass instruments, resulting in what has been referred to as "newgrass."

Aside from specific instrumentation, a distinguishing characteristic of bluegrass is vocal harmony featuring two, three, or four parts, often with a sound in the highest voice, a style described as the "high, lonesome sound." Commonly, the ordering and layering of vocal harmony is called the 'stack'. A standard stack has a baritone voice at the bottom, the lead in the middle (singing the main melody) and a tenor at the top; although stacks can be altered, especially where a female voice is included. Alison Krauss and Union Station provide a good example of a different harmony stack with a baritone and tenor with a high lead, an octave above the standard melody line, sung by the female vocalist. However, by employing variants to the standard trio vocal arrangement, they were simply following a pattern existing since the early days of the genre. The Stanley Brothers utilized a high baritone part on several of their trios recorded for Columbia records during their time with that label (1950-1953). Mandolin player Pee Wee Lambert sang the high baritone above Ralph Stanley's tenor, both parts above Carter's lead vocal. This trio vocal arrangement was variously used by other groups as well. In the 1960's Flatt and Scruggs often added a fifth part to the traditional quartet parts on gospel songs, the extra part being a high baritone (doubling the baritone part sung in the normal range of that voice; Howard Watts (aka 'Cedric Rainwater providing the part). The use of a high lead with the tenor and baritone below it was most famously employed by the Osborne Brothers who first employed it during their time with MGM records in the latter half of the 1950's. This vocal arrangement would be the defining aspect of the Osbornes' sound with Bobby's high, clear voice at the top of the vocal stack.

Bluegrass tunes can largely be described as narratives on the everyday lives of the people from whence the music came. Aside from laments about loves lost, interpersonal tensions and unwanted changes to the region (e.g., the visible effects of mountaintop coal mining), bluegrass vocals frequently reference the hard-scrabble existence of living in Appalachia and other rural areas with modest financial resources. Some protest music has been composed in the bluegrass style, especially concerning the vicissitudes of the Appalachian coal mining industry. Railroading has also been a popular theme, with ballads such as "Wreck of the Old 97" and "Nine Pound Hammer" (from the legend of John Henry) being exemplary. There are also songs about the weather, mostly about rain, for example,"No Place to Hide" and "Early Morning Rain"

Chapter 3 - Bluegrass Gospel Jam Culture Defined

"Bluegrass gospel" has emerged as a subgenre of Traditional Bluegrass. Many bluegrass artists incorporate gospel music into their repertoire. Distinctive elements of this style include Christian lyrics, soulful three- or four-part harmony singing, and sometimes playing subdued instrumentals. Mainstream bluegrass artists Doyle Lawson & Quicksilver and IIIrd Tyme Out have produced bluegrass gospel music. While The Issacs, Mount Zion and The Churchmen play Bluegrass Gospel exclusively.

Gospel Music is music that is written to express either personal, spiritual or a communal belief regarding Christian life, as well as (in terms of the varying music styles) to give a Christian alternative to mainstream secular music. Like other forms of Christian music, the creation, performance, significance, and even the definition of gospel music varies according to culture and social context. Gospel music is composed and performed for many purposes, including aesthetic pleasure, religious or ceremonial purposes, and as an entertainment product for the marketplace. However, a theme of gospel music is praise, worship or thanks to God, Christ, or the Holy Spirit. Gospel music in general is characterized by dominant vocals (often with strong use of harmony) referencing lyrics of a religious nature, particularly Christian. Subgenres include contemporary gospel, urban contemporary gospel (sometimes referred to as "black gospel"), Southern gospel, and modern gospel music (now more commonly known as praise and worship music or contemporary Christian music). Several forms of gospel music utilize choirs, use piano or Hammond organ, drums, bass guitar and, increasingly, electric guitar. In comparison with hymns, which are generally of a statelier measure, the *gospel song* is expected to have a refrain and often a more syncopated rhythm.

Some proponents of "standard" hymns generally dislike gospel music of the late 19th and early 20th centuries. For example, Patrick and Syndor complain that commercial success led to a proliferation of such music, and "deterioration, even in a standard which to begin with was not high, resulted." They went on to say, "there is no doubt that a deterioration in taste follows the use of this type of hymn and tune; it fosters an attachment to the trivial and sensational which dulls and often destroys sense of the dignity and beauty which best befit the song that is used in the service of God."

Gold reviewed the issue in 1958, and collected a number of quotations similar to the complaints of Patrick and Syndor. However, he also provided this quotation: "Gospel hymnody has the distinction of being America's most typical contribution to Christian song. As such, it is valid in its inspiration and in its employment." (Robert Stevenson, *Religion in Life*, Winter, 1950-51.)

Today, with historical distance, there is a greater acceptance of such gospel songs into official denominational hymnals. In the preface, the editors say, "Experience has shown that some older treasures were missed when the current hymnals were compiled," a diplomatic way of saying, "It's all right to sing these songs in church."

The Bluegrass Gospel Jam Culture is unique in several ways. First, the music is usually spontaneous. Whenever musicians gather, they enjoy playing the music and taking turns. They demonstrate to each other different strums and picking styles. The unique tradition is that they share their songs and music simply because they want to. In other musical circles, the audiences have to *"go"* and *"pay"* to hear performances. Bluegrass Gospel Jam players simply go to play and have fun performing with other musicians.

Chapter 4 - Two Kinds Of Jams

"Par versus Per" (Participation Versus Performance)

From the outset, my personal passion has been to invite and encourage beginner participants to come, learn, and to have fun.

Over the years, I have found that many people have instruments stowed away somewhere. There simply has been no outlet or venue in which to share musical abilities. The Jams offer exceptional opportunities for musicians to rediscover and improve skills that have been dormant for a long time.

I encourage beginners and experienced performers to play together for the benefit of all. The combination is an awesome harmonious experience. Along with active audience participation, marvelous melodies emerge in mind-blowing unison and harmony. It all starts when participant beginner musicians join in.

When performers gather together in a public place and play in front of an audience, they have all mutually agreed to cooperate in making music together. Performers who practice over and over are seeking professional status. In Bluegrass Gospel Jams, musical skills of all levels are represented. Most everyone is in a high active learning mode. *Participation is the key.*

Participation is emphasized over performance.

Everyone gets a chance. A comfortable and welcoming spirit settles in. Newly composed original songs by jam musicians are now showing up. Smiles emanate from the audience. Laughter bursts out in between the songs. A whole lot of camaraderie happens spontaneously. New friendships develop quickly. Everyone, audience and musicians, have a good time. The fifteen-minute breaks in the middle of the jams provide opportunity to mutually participate and mingle even more. I grasp the opportunity to meet, greet, and welcome new folks.

Have you, or someone you have known, ever been the basketball player *(the bench warmer)* who is on the team, but never gets to play? A Bluegrass Gospel Jam gives the *"bench warmers"* an *"on the go"* opportunity to play and develop. Just as in the waning moments of a tense basketball game, the better players foul out, and the players on the bench step up and play, usually better than ever before. In a Jam, it's called *"joining in."*

By design, musicians, when encouraged and given the opportunity, play their heart out. This is a unique tradition that we want to continually grow and foster. I'm not opposed to seeing performers perform perfectly. I enjoy those performances, too. I just realize there are a lot of sideline and backup people out there who can step up and make a few baskets, and still be a more active member of a team. The magic of the Jams is that performers and participants both share in the active distribution of the gospel through bluegrass gospel music.

World Wide Passion

Bluegrass musicians are everywhere. Bluegrass music offers a wide scope in the type of music that is played. Bluegrass music is a distinct style that has evolved from other forms of music. The biggest difference is that bluegrass musicians simply enjoy gathering together to play for fun. Whenever a jam is announced, musicians show up. It could be described as a huge group of musicians (who usually don't know each other yet) having fun while they practice and encourage one another. As a result, Bluegrass Gospel Jam groups rapidly develop.

Isaiah 52: 7
How beautiful on the mountains are the feet of those who bring good news, who proclaim peace, who bring good tidings, who proclaim salvation, who say to Zion, Your God reigns.

Audience Participation

Bluegrass Gospel Jams include sharing participation with the audiences. By allowing both the audience and band members to choose individual songs, I find that everyone contributes. What I like most is that everyone tries. When an audience member chooses a particular song, I sometimes invite that person to come up front and sing with us. I can usually recruit some friends seated beside that person to come up and help. We offer a welcoming and encouraging environment. We generate laughter and smiles.

In a small town close to Douglas, Wyoming, we were attempting to get a new jam started in the basement of a small church. Even though no formal advertising attempts had been made, the small surrounding towns seemed to communicate with each other. Many new musicians gathered together to play. The Jam proceeded well. I got three younger teenager girl singers to come up front with us. Even though they had not performed together as a group, the musicians and the girls blended superbly together. *("That's the true definition of a Bluegrass Gospel Jam.")*

At one of the audience song selection times, the mother of one of the girls picked out a song for us to perform. I was the leader. I encouraged the mother to come up front and join in. She was sitting in the last row of chairs. She refused to come up, shaking her head, *"No!"* I went after her. I left the leadership position and went back and grabbed her hand and encouraged her to come up front. Everyone was laughing at the spectacle. I literally started dragging her towards the front, the lady in one hand, and my guitar in my other hand. She adamantly stated, *"I'll die if I get up there!"*

As I tugged and pulled, I announced to the Gospel Jam crowd, *"Pastor, I would like to let you know that there will be a funeral immediately after the Jam. This lady said she was going to die!"*

Laughter ensued the hilarious situation. She did not die! She sang two songs with us. She shook her head back and forth on the way back to her seat. She was smiling and relieved and exhausted from all the effort it took to go up front. Now, however, the audience members were more reluctant to select a song. *"I wonder why?"* When the attitude is friendly and welcoming, more folks become involved.

I rely on God's guidance when I sense that the timing is right to call forth a stranger to join in. It's just another unique way I obtain participation. By joining in, a musician plays and sings far better than he or she ever has. It's amazing to watch participation turn into performance. Why? We are sharing the gospel with anyone who drops in.

"Try Principle"

At first encounter, almost everyone I meet always apologizes for his or her shortcomings as a musician or singer. I have learned to look beyond those statements. I know the potential is there, ready to be unleashed by a gentle or firm nudge. I have uncovered that even the best musicians are reluctant to join in. Everyone seems to think they have to be better than they are right now. They seem to always be worrying about how they will appear if they make some mistakes in front of an audience. I have discovered that two suggestions make the difference:

(1) The musicians have to have an invitation to *"try."*

(2) The musicians need and want the *"encouragement nudge."*

At first, most of the new arrival musicians and singers join in on the sidelines before they come further up front.

That gives me the opportunity to meet them on a personal basis. I lead the Jam, but I also mingle with the audiences and arriving musicians. I welcome them, find out their name, thank them for coming, and encourage them in any way I can. I try to make their visit friendly and enjoyable.

We don't condemn anyone for playing wrong notes or making mistakes during the songs. We march on and keep trying to the best of our abilities. This welcoming spirit permeates. The *"Try Principle"* is the *prominent and dominant underlying concept of the bluegrass gospel jams.*

Encouraging Beginner Musicians

I encourage beginner musicians all of the time. The jams are built on beginner encouragement. I first encourage musicians (and audiences) to bring their instrument. We provide seats on the outside walls of the semicircle so that new musician participants can sit on the fringes of the jam before they gain more confidence to *"officially join in."*

We have start-up songbooks with chords and words so everyone can more easily join in.

Instrument Workshops are an excellent way for beginners to become connected. We offer the beginner musicians the start-up songbooks they can purchase and take home to practice.

I smile. I welcome them in. I learn their name.

Encouraging Intermediate Musicians

Why musicians keep their musical skills hidden is an absolute mystery to me. Part of my most enjoyable leadership task is to uncover and bring forth those hidden skills.

I have found that musicians love to play together. They learn from each other. They joke around a lot. In short, they have a good time. A Bluegrass Gospel Jam is really just a big party where everyone gets to participate. Intermediate musicians love to learn new songs and strums. All you have to do is give them a location where they can gather and play. They encourage one another.

Encouraging Rusty Musicians

"Rusty" musicians are my other favorite. I enjoy *"reviving"* musicians who used to play, but don't seem to find the time any more. There is normally no place for them to go to play. We provide the locations.

Instruments often reside in forlorn closets, garages, or basements, all gathering dust. As soon as these *"haven't played in a long time"* musicians drop in on a Jam, their emotions are stirred. *"Memories"* start attracting them in.

"Rusty" musicians get to observe and see first-hand that they are welcome to join in with the fun. They do need extra encouragement. They do have to be actually invited by someone. Every time a musician comes in, he or she brings other family members and friends. That's the underlying secret of Jam expansion.

Encouraging Performer Musicians

Not much encouragement is needed for performer musicians to show up. Performer musicians drift in, almost without human intervention. They just enjoy having available, a public place to perform. The Jams act like a magnet to attract musicians. Performer musicians begin bonding with the other musicians. Musical harmony emanates instinctively. Performer musicians and beginner musicians begin blending together.

Encouraging Small Performer Groups

I encourage the startup of small circle jams at someone's house. I also encourage the musicians to find other venues where they can play and sing as a small group, such as café's and senior home centers. These smaller locations offer more opportunities to perform. They provide outreach environments in which to share.

Let the musicians know that you will help advertise their event. Help the musicians understand that individual gospel jams are not competing with each other. In fact this is a healthy outcome. We are all working harmoniously in spreading the gospel wherever we can.

Often, other churches will invite the whole Jam to come and play. I say *"Yes"* to the invitation before I ever present the idea to the Jam members. My only primary rule is that the proposed location be no more than an hour away from our Bluegrass Gospel Jam home base. Having food available is a masterful drawing card. We enjoy, *"playing for our dinner."*

Isaiah 26: 3

You will keep in perfect peace him whose mind is steadfast, because he trusts in you. Trust in the Lord forever, for the Lord, the Lord, is the rock eternal.

"Ron's Rule Of Participation Explained"

The bluegrass gospel jam is the starting place for musicians. *"Come as you are,"* is the underlying fundamental objective. *We practice as we play!* We encourage as we perform. We blend into the gospel spirit. We are the launching pad for both beginning and intermediate musicians. Maybe without realizing it, experienced performers help lead and guide the way. We all perform better as we practice. Audiences enjoy the relaxed encouraging ambiance. *"Participation makes all the difference."*

Where can someone go and just show up and play along? Yes, it's the Bluegrass Gospel Jam that allows and heartens the connection. The whole design of the Gospel Jams is designed to allow involvement. Youngsters are also encouraged to come up and join in.

Proverbs 14: 30

A heart at peace gives life to the body, but envy rots the bones.

Patricia's Problem

Patricia was one of the performer musicians who first joined up with the Bluegrass Gospel Jam. Patricia had even produced a CD. We had been given permission to do a short abbreviated jam with puppets and songs during the church service for the kids. During the prior week, as we tried to construct a performance, we were rehearsing.

Patricia came up to me and made the statement, *"Ron, these singers and musicians are all off key and rhythm."*

"Well, I don't really have any way to correct that situation. All we have are volunteer musicians who are trying. We will have to do with what we have."

"Ron, you can't do that! When you are playing in God's house (the church), you have to perform the songs perfectly! Nothing else will do!"

"Well, Patricia, I guess we will have to agree that we disagree on that point! These musicians are trying and we are far from being perfect. We are not as talented as you are."

Patricia wasn't happy with the outcome of that discussion, but she showed up on the Sunday of our performance. Patricia didn't perform in the regular program, but I talked her into being the voice of one of the puppets singing one of the songs. We put Patricia behind the puppet stage, and the song came out beautifully. At the end of our *"imperfect performance,"* everyone in the congregation clapped and applauded. No one mentioned how we were *"off key"* and *"off rhythm."* They all enjoyed us because we tried to the best of our abilities. Ron's other minor rule is, *"You don't have to be the best before you perform. But you do need to be given the opportunity once in a while in the appropriate environment."*

What's The Difference?

In front of a church congregation, if you were to ask the question, *"How many of you know how to sing? Please raise your hands."* Not many would respond. If you asked a subsequent follow-up question, *"How many of you know how to sing in harmony?"* Very few hands would go up.

"Then, why does a song sound so beautiful when we sing together as a congregation?"

That's right, we are all doing our part, singing along. God orchestrates the music in our hearts and souls and voices. It all blends beautifully when each of us does our part. Whether *"off key,"* or *"on key,"* that's what happens at the bluegrass gospel jams. We participate and offer opportunities to grow into becoming better. Do you know what the difference is between a performer and a participant? Practice!

Instruments In The Trunk

At the beginning of each jam, as soon as the audience begins arriving, I announce, *"Does anyone have an instrument out in their car or trunk?"*

I always smile and say; *"You know that's not good for an instrument to be out there all alone."*

Often the musicians will go out and bring the instrument inside. Within minutes, they join in, too.

Chapter 5 - Be A Bluegrass Gospel Jam Musician

How to be a Bluegrass Gospel Jam Musician

- Just show up
- Attend Instrument Workshops
- Attend Bluegrass Gospel Festivals
- Have courage
- Attend any kind of bluegrass jam gathering
- Watch the fingers of the musician next to you
- Buy a Capo
- Buy a chromatic tuner
- Learn the words to the songs being played
- Learn which word upon which the song chord changes to another finger position

Confidence Building Techniques

- Encouragement to try
- Patience in learning
- Sharing musical abilities with others
- Courage to start

Fear Factors Identified

- First time playing an instrument
- First time singing into a microphone
- First time playing with a group
- First time performing in front of an audience
- First time playing a new song
- First time writing a new original song
- First time starting up a new Bluegrass Gospel Jam
- First time fully trusting God for the outcomes
- First time actually praying

Isaiah 26: 3

You will keep in perfect peace him whose mind is steadfast, because he trusts in you. Trust in the Lord forever, for the Lord, the Lord, is the rock eternal.

At The Beginning

At age 61, when I first had the urge to play a guitar, I very much wanted to participate in a bluegrass jam. Most of the early bluegrass jams I attended were groups of very skilled musicians who would not let me into their inner circle. I was always excluded because I was a beginner. Those early bluegrass musicians played primarily non-gospel songs. They were excellent musicians playing all to themselves. They were a closed circle jam who ignored any spectators who were present.

Beginner Participation

I decided to turn this situation around. I began creating an environment where we played predominately gospel songs. I especially encouraged beginner participation. I made the rule that the jam musicians could not turn their backs to the audience. I began encouraging the members of the audience to choose songs. I encouraged musicians, whether experienced or beginner, to take turns choosing the songs. I searched and found physical locations where there was adequate room and parking for both musicians and audiences.

Why Do It?

I believe that God's word gets *"spread"* through the medium of bluegrass gospel music. I believe that the Holy Spirit is present at the jams, spreading peace among the midst of musicians and spectators. *"God's word never returns void. It accomplishes the purpose of why God sent it."*

I believe that the jams offer a respite for tired travelers who don't take time to go to church. The jams are a ministry to folks who might not believe in God. I believe that the jams offer camaraderie and fellowship in a unique peaceable environment of gospel music. Gospel songs proclaim who God is. Music is a healing balm that helps comfort folks with the daily problems of everyday life.

Sense Of Purpose

As in any volunteer gathering, participants have to learn to get along together. Musicians are each individual artists. Over the years, I have found that most musicians I encounter are usually already talented. Even though talented to some degree, they still have to be encouraged to come and join in. The biggest challenges occur when the musicians, beginner or experienced, feel they have to be *"perfect"* before they join in. The jam is a place to learn, share, and have fun while learning.

When a musician finally grasps the concept that the music is not about the individual musician or song, but rather an encouragement for the audience and other musician attendees, a sense of purpose begins to emerge.

Do What You Can With What You Have

With no talent, no musical ability, and no money, I started a gospel jam out of nothing. I did the one smart thing. I turned over to God, all of the gospel jams. I still do what I can with what I have. That's my obligation, my part. God is supplying all the increase. Can a simple idea like a Bluegrass Gospel Jam turn into a witness for God? *"Yes, it's happening as we speak, sing, play, and fellowship."*

All Experience Levels

New musicians, intermediate musicians, and *"rusty"* musicians are all encouraged. Experienced performer musicians are encouraged. Sometimes during the songs, discordant keys, and discordant melodies, stand out along with other mistakes. We keep going anyway. We allow the participants, and the performers, to make mistakes. God did not say, *"Be thou perfect before thou canst join in!"* No, God says, *"Come as you are!"* Together, we have a powerful impact with our fellow musicians and our listening and participating audiences.

Bluegrass Gospel Music Fans

- Everyone always welcome
- Family friendly safe environment
- Hear good old favorite gospel songs
- Wholesome activities to invite and attend with friends
- Based on principles of peace… always relaxing
- Walk away being encouraged enough to invite other friends to the next jam.

Psalm 29: 11

The Lord gives strength to his people; the Lord blesses his people with peace.

Beginner Guitar Lessons

At one of the early Jams, I offered half-hour *"Beginner Guitar Lessons"* right before the jam started. Sharon started bringing her granddaughter for the free lessons. Then Sharon would disappear until the lesson was over. Sharon never stayed around for the rest of the Jam. One night she picked up one of the booklets I had written, *"The Pursuit Of Peace, Living As If I Were Rich."* Seven months later, she sent me an email stating how much that booklet had affected and helped her during some troublesome times she was going through.

Soon Sharon started coming regularly to the Jams. She was one of the performer musicians who came along and started joining into the participation effect. She became encouraged. Sharon started writing and performing her own original songs.

Shy In The Background

In the early Jams, Karen was shy and always lingering in the background. She never took a turn choosing a song. She always *"passed"* when her turn came to choose a song. She was quiet, but she always lugged in four different instruments. Every once in a while, I could hear her violin playing clearly and concisely. She never chose to take an instrumental break. When asked during a song, she just smiled and shook her head, *"No."* She was just a hushed participator.

On one Jam day, about a year later, she came in and delivered to me an entire CD with songs she had composed and performed. I had no idea she was so talented. She was just a reserved and unassuming personality. As the Jams progressed,

I began energizing my efforts to have her exhibit more and more of her talents. Like a beautiful damsel butterfly emerging out of a cocoon, she became more and more active. She also invited and attracted more musician friends and families to come and join in. She is still an avid participator.

Becky

I often receive criticisms when I allow a new person to come up and enter in with the Jam. Often, that new person has very little or no musical ability. I don't hold an audition before that person comes up to a microphone. I figure that if someone has the courage to come up, that I have the courage to encourage him or her.

Becky is about ten years old. She came up on stage to sing a couple of times. Right now, she can't carry a tune. Her singing is actually loud and awful. At the last Jam, beside me, she was playing a washboard with two sticks. Even with my non-experienced ears, I could tell that she couldn't keep the beat. I pondered on whether or not I should actively encourage her.

After the refreshment break, Becky came back up on the stage. She was curious about Dixie's Q-Chord (an electric autoharp.) Dixie was demonstrating to Becky. All of sudden, as Becky's fingers floated up and down the Q-Chord keyboard, I heard melodious songs coming forth. Becky was already learning the new instrument. She was catching on, fast. I made sure that I mentioned to her mother, Becky's new skill with the Q-Chord. I hope that Becky's mom will be able to purchase a new Q-Chord for Becky. *"You never know what can happen by encouraging someone, whether young, or old, talented or not."* **Who's Next?**

Simplify The Plan

What's the secret to starting up a Bluegrass Gospel Jam?

- Receptive and creative open mind.
- *"Gather together and make music together."*

Chapter 6 - Starting A Bluegrass Gospel Jam

The Evans Jam

Some time back, we held an inaugural Jam in a small town called Evans, Colorado, just south of Greeley. The hostess, Joanne, first contacted me after she saw the Gospel Jam website. She had also attended a couple of previous jams about one and a half years earlier. Joanne tracked my phone number down and called me and emailed me about starting up a bluegrass gospel jam at her small church. We set up a coffee meeting time.

Joanne asked for and received approval and encouragement from the church congregation to host the Bluegrass Gospel Jam event.

On a second coffee time, I invited Dean and Darlene to join us. Dean & Darlene were willing to bring their sound system and help jump-start the Jam. This was my choice because I knew that bringing the sound system was an integral part of Dean & Darlene's personal participation ministry. Also the situation allowed Dean and Darlene to participate in the planning of an event from start to finish. We went over to Joanne's church and checked out the facilities of the room we would be using.

We chose a date on the first Saturday of March, about six weeks away. Joanne was reluctant to start that soon. She figured it would take much more time to gather musicians together. I encouraged her to start right away and I encouraged her that God would send whomever was supposed to come. She followed my lead and experience.

The outcome was absolutely phenomenal. I started advertising the new jam in my weekly email newsletter. Joanne placed an advertisement in the Greeley newspaper.

Joanne's goal, *"Our church is the best kept secret around. Let's do something to put our church on the map!"*

The Evans Church was approximately 40 minutes away from our primary home-base location. The turnout was overflowing and bountiful. Musicians and audience came from as far as 1 1/2 hours away. At one early count, we had 21 musicians and 68 spectators packed into a fellowship room. Others kept filing in. We had to continually set up more folding chairs. Steve car-pooled with me.

On the way to the church, Joanne had placed a sandwich sign off the main street with an arrow pointing south to the Bluegrass Gospel Jam. We brought in eight new songbooks to pass around to musicians. The music was totally awesome. The audience resounded spontaneously. That little church bulged with gospel music. We also performed a few requested non-gospel songs.

Every musician received an opportunity to choose a song. Some got to choose two songs. The audience also made song requests. We were able to accommodate each audience request. I was up front at center stage. Nora passed notes to me with the audience song requests. She took many digital pictures. We ran over the time limit because we were having such a good time. At the break in the middle, Joanne and the church members served sandwiches, snacks, coffee, and water to all the musicians and spectators. All the spectators remained. No one left after the break. They were having an enjoyable good time.

As the Jam progressed, I looked around at the audience's faces. Every person was singing along... every person. I began mingling with the audience, adjusting the musician volume up so every person could hear. It was simply a joyous occasion for everyone. This was Joanne's first Jam. It was a huge joint effort and accomplishment.

Musicians from all the Northern Colorado area continued to show up. This Jam was definitely a personal victory for me. I was the catalyst to get the Gospel Jam started. It was like we climbed to this pinnacle of a mountain top experience. I got to see firsthand the results from overcoming all the struggles, setbacks, challenges, and discouraging times.

Joanne is now reserving the City Park so we can do an outdoor concert in late summer. She is excited and amazed at all the possibilities. She was literally, almost *"blown away"* by the unexpected and overwhelming positive response.

"Oh, I did personally pray that morning for God to send the people God wanted to come!"

Startup Chronicle Timeline

This Evans Jam was a primary example of all my efforts to get Jams started up all over the USA. Follow the timeline.

- November:
    - Joanne found the Bluegrass Gospel Jam website. She called me and sent me an email requesting my help to start up a Jam at her church.

- December:
    - We met for coffee and talked one-on-one.
    - I started advertising in my weekly email newsletter, the proposed opening of a new Jam in the Evans/Greeley area.

- January:
    - Joanne received permission from her church to host the Jam event.

- February:

- o Joanne, Dean, Darlene, and I met for a second coffee appointment at the Double Clutch Café in Evans.

- o Joanne placed an advertisement in the Greeley newspaper.

- o She also placed posters at grocery stores and other businesses. She mailed invitations to the music stores.

- o She made phone calls to friends and promoted the Jam to the church members.

- o I sent Joanne an email *"Start-Up Kit"* to assist with rosters, brochure ideas, flyer promotion, and suggestions for holding a successful Jam.

- March 3

    - o The Jam was a rousing success.

From the beginning to the conclusion, a new Jam emerged in just three months... from an idea, to a full-blown success. All my experiences over the years worked together like clockwork to cause the Jam to come to mutual fruition. And the real reason the Jam came together was because from the *"Get-Go,"* we all turned the whole idea over to God.

Maine To Florida To Massachusetts

"Why don't you offer to sell musician CDs at your Jams on a consignment basis?" Norman asked. *"Then you could also set the stage for selling your books at the Jams."*

When my first published books came out, I was reluctant to sell my "Pursuit Of Peace" books at the Jams. I didn't want people to think I was holding the Jams just to merchandise my books. This was an erroneous thinking pattern that I maintained for some time. So when Norman made the suggestion, I went ahead with the CD consignment plan. I had already inputted a large email address list of Bluegrass Gospel Musicians from a *"GospelGrass"* flyer I picked up at a Bluegrass Gospel Festival. At the same time, we had been in contact with Wendel, a musician in Maine. He wanted to get his personal performance CD distributed. We ended up making a $100 investment to purchase a box of Wendel's CDs to remarket at the Bluegrass Gospel Jams.

I began sending out emails to the GospelGrass musician bands proposing that we also market their CDs on a consignment basis, with a small profit going to the Jam. I had the performer musicians send me a sample CD so I could preview the music before sponsoring the CD at the Jams. When the songs were acceptable (I didn't have any that weren't acceptable), I requested that the bands send me ten CDs. I then began marketing the CDs for the bands.

The plan worked well for a time. I had about 25 musicians sending me their CDs. Bookkeeping and tracking sales soon became too tedious for the small amount of revenue. Eventually, I made the hard decision to return the unsold CDs.

Brooksville, Florida

Wendel, from Maine, told Cheryl from Florida, that, *"Ron would help market Cheryl's CDs."* After marketing Cheryl's CDs for a few months, she became interested in the Bluegrass Gospel Jam concept. Eventually, I was able to fly down to Brooksville, and help inaugurate Cheryl's new Jam. The Brooksville Jam is still up and running. It all started when I initiated making email contacts with musician bands.

Plainview, Massachusetts

Chuck also discovered the Bluegrass Gospel Jam website and contacted me immediately. He wanted to start up a Jam at his church every other Thursday evening. He wanted to get started as soon as possible. I immediately emailed the *"start-up kit"* that he purchased. Because of the website, we became friends. We had lots of email communication and phone conversations. He has experienced many of the obstacles I experienced, but through diligence, the Massachusetts Jam continues to grow. He sent me a video of himself and his Jam members playing on a *"flat-bed trailer"* in a parade down his town's main street. Chuck sends me a periodic *"update email."* I include his comments on the email *"Weekly Update Newsletter"* that I send out every Wednesday of the week.

Sterling, Colorado

John Horner was searching the Internet for Bluegrass Gospel Jams when he also found our Bluegrass Gospel Jam website. I helped him get started. His Jam started playing every other Sunday afternoon at the Senior Center and is still continuing.

John and I get together for lunch every few months and share gospel jam stories.

Home Base Fort Collins, Colorado

From our home base in Fort Collins, Colorado, Bluegrass Gospel Jams have flourished. Once folks attend, they have a burning desire to start up their own jams in other locations. Right now, as of this printing, we currently have over nine Jam locations. By the time you read this book, we fully expect to expand to over fifty locations in fifty states. I should say; *"musicians are attracting new locations."* We go wherever we think God is leading. It's amazing to me to recognize the power of a local Jam to reach musicians of all skills. My task is to plant the *"Mustard Seeds of Faith,"* and encourage each new Jam leader to make their Jam become self-sufficient, but still under God's guidance.

2 Thessalonians 3: 16

Now may the Lord of peace himself give you peace at all times and in every way...

Benefits From Forming A Bluegrass Gospel Jam

I believe that I am on a mission for God. It's an easy way for me to share my faith with others. I have become a better encourager. My target audience is fringe believers and beginner believers. I also get the opportunity to encourage musicians who haven't played for a long time. I call these musicians, "*rusty musicians.*" I encourage these old-time players to bring their instruments out of storage and rediscover their musician skills.

Outcome Thinking

With God in control, God will help guide your thinking and planning time. What do you want the outcome to be? Be careful, you will probably receive what you are thinking about all day long. Your thoughts will change as you have new learning experiences. It's never to late to begin again.

New thoughts, combined with God's guidance, can make you into a new, and better person. Outcome thinking is uncovering the strategic faith path that God is spreading out for you to follow. Which is best? Is it your way? Is it God's way? All God really wants is for you to have courage to take the first step and then rely on his help. A prayer followed by a step forward is a terrific way to begin. Don't worry. You will receive course corrections all along the way.

Trust and believe.

Take God-inspired action.

My Personal Core Value

"This is not Ron's Jam. It is God's Jam."

I Always Pray This Prayer On The Morning Of Each Jam

"Lord I pray, that even right now, at this late hour, that you will send the people you want to come to this jam."

Partnership Deal With God

"I do the inviting and encouraging. God takes care of sending the people. How many people come, is not my problem. That's God's problem."

My Part Is To Invite

"I just don't worry at all about how many, or who, will come to the jam. God has lifted off my shoulders, all the pressure of trying to figure everything out in advance. It's a joyous feeling. My part is to invite and show up. God does all the rest."

Write down on paper *your reasons* for wanting to start a bluegrass gospel jam.

My reasons:

- The desire to play gospel music was within me.

- I wanted to demonstrate that Christians could have fun.

- I wanted to encourage non-believers to come to church.

- I wanted to create an atmosphere where people could slow down, relax, and have a fun family time in a safe welcoming environment.

- I wanted to create a place where beginners could begin to learn and practice their skills.

- I wanted to emphasize participation over performance.

Helpful Hint

Locate A Local Bluegrass Jam. Search out other bluegrass and country jams. Begin consistent attendance. Participation is the quickest way to learn, improve, and polish skills. Most of the time, I attended a jam every Sunday afternoon. The first people who came to the bluegrass gospel jams were spectators and musicians I first met at the regular *"bluegrass jams."*

Ron's Second Rule Of Participation

"God will send the people… if you will do the inviting and encouraging."

Communication Diligence (Email)

Email is my one primary source of communication.

Three things to think about when dealing with people on email:

- Most of the folks don't take time to read the email
- Most of the time folks don't forward the email to friends
- Most of the time, folks won't respond to let the leader know if they are attending or not.

Regardless of the lack of prompt reply communication, musicians and spectators from everywhere still show up on the day of the jam. Operating a bluegrass gospel jam is definitely *"a faith plan put into action."*

Email Header Marketing

Place the actual core of your email message in the *"subject line,"* so that the information in the message is immediately transmitted to the email recipient. Even if that person doesn't take time to read, right away, the whole email message, the primary message is clearly communicated in the subject line. Be brief and to the point. Always send out promptly, to each new attendee, a *"welcome"* email.

Become An Expert Email Coordinator

At each jam, begin gathering email addresses. Pass around a clipboard with an email roster form. Use large space lines for everyone to write down **(*Print Clearly!*)** his or her name and email address. Mailing addresses and phone numbers aren't needed if they never get used.

Every week, email consistently to both spectators and musicians. I now send out an updated newsletter every Wednesday.

Create a specific grouping list for specialized mailings to musicians.

Always choose your email wording in a positive manner. In every email, include the same invitation message as on your index-card marketing piece. That way, every person who receives your email receives a continual invitation.

Encourage the email recipients to forward the email to friends and family who might be interested in coming. Look forward to contacting *"people you haven't even met yet."* Staying in touch with a lot of different folks is always a tremendous challenge. Email contact is the most efficient method. On the week preceding the immediate upcoming Jam, email at least two or three times during the week.

Psalm 29: 11

The Lord gives strength to his people; the Lord blesses his people with peace.

What Days Work Best For Jams?

We have tried Sunday nights, Saturday nights, and even Thursday nights. We have tried every other week, and once a month venues. For now, the best outcomes have occurred on Saturday afternoons, once a month, from 12:00 to 4:00. Each new leader individually orchestrates the time and place of the new jam gatherings. I have found that musicians will come, stay, and play as long as you will allow them. Musicians thrive on making music together. Having a consistent location, day, and time allows musicians to schedule in and participate in a Bluegrass Gospel Jam.

What Kind Of Faith Should A Leader Maintain?

Just this morning at breakfast, I had to remind myself that the Jam coming this Saturday is under God's control, and for me to not be concerned about something that is entirely built on faith. What a relief! Don't worry about not having enough faith. Faith will develop as quickly as the leader will allow faith to develop!

Chapter 7 - Leading A Bluegrass Gospel Jam

Primary Emotions That Surface

As a new venture, when you first begin leading a gospel jam, let me share some of the emotions you might experience. I used to watch half hour singing groups on TV, especially country western groups. At the end of the programs, it seemed like the group always played a religious song.

All I really did was to reverse that pattern. We play gospel songs first, and regular or non-gospel songs second. This could be a new emotional concept for you. It was for me. But the success was awesome. I didn't have forethought and a plan and schedule to organize a big gathering of musicians. When you are trying something new, everyone feels apprehensions. I felt scared. You, too, will probably experience fear. Expect it.

Shift The Focus

I enjoy the challenge of getting musicians to focus on the audience rather than upon themselves. In many ways, musicians are almost always the same. At first they are reluctant to get up front and play a song. They feel inadequate to perform. *I encourage performing without regard to being perfect.*

My focus is on others. My focus is on faith in God. God helps me play my guitar, sing, perform, and encourage. God gives me extra strength and courage. As the leader of the Bluegrass Gospel Jam, I am a witness for God. By becoming a bluegrass gospel jam leader, you can also encompass that same benefit.

Love The People

How will they know we are Christians? *"By our love for one another."* Demonstration and action are more powerful than words. People tend to return to an environment where they are continually learning. Sharing music creates a bond of friendship that glues people's lives together.

Psalm 29: 11

The Lord gives strength to his people; the Lord blesses his people with peace.

It's OK To Start Another Jam

In your strategic planning stage, please put into place, a plan to expand and start over at a new location. As soon as the current location starts becoming packed, encourage another leader to start another Jam. It's OK to start anew, especially if you have planned in advance for that expansion. You can even use the same time and day of the month for the new Jam. Even if the separate jams happen on the same day and same time, the jams do not conflict with one another. Each jam location has a unique and different personality with a distinct and inimitable following.

Many times, leaders think that there isn't enough room for another jam in the same community. That's because those leaders are not thinking large enough. In this book, you will find the story of how I felt that way, too. I almost quit having the jams because my feelings were hurt. I found that by taking a three-month *"personal-time"* short vacation, I regained my fervor for the Jams. When I felt that God was encouraging me to go again, I started a new jam in a new location. During that self-imposed *"time off,"* I did a lot of thinking and talking with God. I had a new focus. As my thinking and waiting time sifted through all summer, I began feeling that God wanted the Jams to continue.

I started out again, with new musicians, at a new central location, at the church I was attending. The temporary setback I experienced was an extremely painful experience for me. I now believe I am headed in a more powerful and better direction. Here is an appropriate encouragement email I just received this morning.

"Nothing great was ever achieved without enthusiasm." Ralph Waldo Emerson

Overcoming Discouragement

I recommend surrounding yourself with well-chosen supporters who believe in the principles of the gospel jam concept. One griper or complainer can adversely affect the outcomes you are seeking. Try not to be completely alone.

I suggest you also make personal peace retreat get-away trips to the mountains, or to a park. Continually ask for God's guidance. Focus on why you do the jams. Focus on the victories.

Take musician general input with a grain of salt. Try to look at problems from above rather than from below. Appreciate the input, but remain dedicated to your principles. Turn the discouragement problems over to God and ask each time, *"OK, God, now how do I handle this situation?"* Wait upon the answer.

Albert Einstein said, *"In the middle of difficulty lies opportunity."*

Mission And Vision

If you could do something specifically for God, what would it be? Could your vision be accomplished through bluegrass gospel music? If you can visualize being on God's team, what position would you play? Do you think God wants *you* to be a leader? Do *you* think you could become a leader?

Can you simply become an encourager, a supporter, or an assistant administrator? There is room for everybody who wants to utilize their talents to help with the outcomes of the Bluegrass Gospel Jams.

Let me ask you a question,

"Do you have to know the outcome before you step out on faith?"

Ron's answer,

"Bottom line...keep on reading the Bible... keep on turning the jams over to God."

Chili/Chocolate Cook Off Event

At our church, we have a fun Saturday night event once each year called, *"A Chili/Chocolate Cook-Off."* Everyone is encouraged to bring a crock-pot of Chili or a luscious chocolate dessert for a potluck supper. There are judges selected to taste each of the Chili recipes and also to sample the chocolate presentations. Prizes for first, second, and third place are awarded. There is a donation bowl for the Deacon's fund that is used to help out folks with financial needs.

Steve, one of the recently participating Bluegrass Gospel Jam musicians, suggested that we do some bluegrass music at the event. Soon we had an impromptu invitation to play for the evening. We made no specific plans on what songs to do. We had no idea of which musicians might come. I sent out an email invitation to the bluegrass gospel jam roster and invited anyone who wanted to come.

We started choosing and playing songs. Our Bluegrass Gospel Jam Songbook played a huge part in generating enthusiasm. We played a lot of bluegrass songs like, *"Your Cheating Heart,"* and *"You Are My Sunshine."* We also played a lot of rousing hand-clapping, toe-tapping, rousing gospel songs. We included, *"Amazing Grace," "I'll Fly Away," "Mansion Over The Hilltop," "How Great Thou Art,"* and *"Unclouded Day."* The audience automatically picked up the emanating spirit. Soon audience members were coming up front and joining in with the singing. This was one of the most fun events we have had. It all started by encouraging people to participate. This is truly a sample of how Bluegrass Gospel Jams take shape. No one worried about how we appeared. We just showed up and shared some music... with fun mixed in.

Sure enough, though, when we musicians took time to partake of the Chili and Chocolate together, one of the chronic complainer musicians (a singer named Jane) began griping loudly about the Jam not having the correct rhythm and melody during the performance.

We had just come from a superb performance generated out of pure participation and enjoyment, without any prior practice. I was at the height of performance as our group played and made excellent music together. And it all started with that simple idea, *"Let's all gather and make music together."*

This event and opportunity was a spontaneous eruption of friendship, fellowship, and fun. And now, here was Jane... complaining. Jane had just finished another of her derogatory remarks. I looked at my chili, I looked at her, and I replied, *"Tough! That's the way it is."*

When I sometimes get off track a little, I have a good friend who uses the expression to me, *"Bunk!"* That's the way I felt about Jane's *"complaining attitude."* On the spot, I reset the tone around that table. Everyone within earshot knew I had taken a stand on why the Jams even exist. I don't believe Jane understands cooperation and encouragement very well. Sometimes it's necessary to make a public statement head-on. It's OK to say, *"Bunk!"* once in a while.

Many times an instrument player or a singer forgets about the learning time it took to get to where they are now. At the Jams, we accommodate the *"let's get started philosophy."* Where would you be if you never received positive encouragement? Simply stated, we are not expecting every song performance to be perfect in all ways. We want to have fun while we are learning.

Stand on your principles in a gentle but firm manner. Manage your emotions. Let God handle your frustrations. Pray for the person doing the offending. Forgive, and you will be forgiven of your own shortcomings.

1 Corinthians: 33

Do not be misled: Bad company corrupts good character.

Matthew 7: 12

"So in everything, do others what you would have them do to you…"

Intentional Process

Hopefully, you will understand that leading a bluegrass gospel jam is an intentional process. It's an opportunity to share with others. If you appreciate the fact that God's word can be shared through music, a gospel jam can easily mature into an *"Outpost Ministry."* It can become a ministry as soon as your thoughts will allow it.

Your specifically stated purpose will determine the mission of the ministry. Most of what I have learned has come from the accidental process. I had no idea that such marvelous outcomes would emerge. That's what happens when we leave the outcomes to God.

Hopefully, these insights I'm sharing with you will give you a head start on pointing you and your new jam in the right direction. God will lead you in ways that are conducive to your own individual spirit and willingness. Are you open to God's leadership? Maybe everything isn't an accidental process. Maybe God knows more than you and I know.

Relational Environment

A Jam is a totally relational environment. It's all about establishing long-term enduring relationships. Almost every musician and every spectator comes because someone they knew, invited them. Yes, with the correct tone and pitch pipe, as the email leader, you are the primary invitation marketing person. The real truth is that folks usually come to a jam because of knowing somebody else who has extended a personal invitation to them.

Email keeps on encouraging and reminding people to come. At least for right now, newspaper or secular methods of advertising are expensive and seldom generate very many attendees. Advertising is important because it does call attention to what is happening. Your email roster is the group to whom you should target your advertising. They, in turn, will invite people they know.

Most folks don't think about how to advertise the Jam to their friends. It's as easy as folks forwarding an email invitation to friends. You have to help them, encourage them, and demonstrate how to become relational. Trying to get people to think about others is one of the huge challenges. You would think that task would be easy. That task is not easy.

You, as the leader, must develop a friendly demeanor with all the folks who come to the jams. The cultivated relational environment has to start at the top and then filter down. When you get to know the names of the musicians and attendees, you know that you are creating the right environment. If you are smiling, others will smile with you. I read in a sales motivation book this statement, *"No salesman ever went broke, who knew the names of his customers' kids."*

"Ice Breakers"

At the Jams, I have the musicians introduce themselves to the audience and tell where they live. I also have the audience introduce themselves individually and tell where they live.

Let the audience know that this grouping of musicians on stage has never practiced together before. *"This is the first time for this particular gathering of musicians. We are in fact, a Jam!"*

Verbally survey the audience. Find out how they first found out about the Jam. The audience will immediately warm up as soon as you purposely begin involving them. The key to early hands-on-successes at every Jam is obtaining audience attention up front. Good schoolteachers, plan in advance, an opening approach. In the same manner, good Jam leaders open with preplanned *"high-quality ice breakers."*

Transparency

"Who you are," is shown by your actions. Regardless of the setbacks and obstacles, I have tried to lead by positive example. However, I have found that I need people to come alongside as assistant leaders. Those assistant leaders are sometimes hard to find. By trial and error, I have agonized and sometimes suffered through those random selection relationships. When a gospel jam leader can share his real feelings with a trusted assistant, solving a problem becomes much easier.

Course corrections can only be made when the real or imagined problems surface. Ignoring situations, or not paying attention to the unseen-but-present, underlying problems, only magnifies the tribulations. Musician *"gossips"* can take the slightest inference or disagreement and turn it into a *"behind-the-scenes raging wildfire."*

People are people, regardless of whether or not they are in a gospel jam group. Please realize that people who gripe and complain are often in a personal transition phase of some kind. Without warning, unbridled opinions or complaints can waylay the leader.

Select assistant leaders who keep you accountable. This is a difficult task when you first start. Yes, the leader needs someone with whom he can be transparent and still function effectively in the leadership role. I have found that, in the volunteer arena, no one seems to want to take on any type of responsibility. On purpose, to help you keep on track, you need to intentionally develop a *"Leadership Guidance Team."*

I Did It Again!

I didn't follow my own advice. At a *"Leadership Guidance Team"* meeting, we decided as a group to *"not hand out"* our newly created Gospel Jam Songbooks for free, as we had previously been doing. It had been discussed and decided that we did not have the funds. We had previously tried offering everything on a *"donation only"* basis. That concept did not work out for us. Sure enough, however, at the next jam, I handed one of the songbooks out free to one of the newer musicians. "*I went against our council of advisors' mutual decision!*" On the next day, we had an event scheduled at another church. This time, when asked, I quoted the price, and collected money in exchange for the songbook.

Let me explain here. In my desires to share and expand the Bluegrass Gospel Jam Outpost Ministry, I have a bad habit of giving away things for free when I don't have the money. Can you relate to that scenario? We are currently working on ways to make the jams become even more self-supporting, just as any business should be. I can't be giving away what I don't have. We have to make wise decisions about how we utilize the funds that do come in, and make sure we are a viable accountability organization. As in any venture, money is needed to operate and expand. I need to continue to operate within wise counsel and practical decision-making. Then I need to personally follow through.

Strategic Planning

Strategic planning meetings provide the groundwork for successful outcomes. Idea implementation is encouraged. Early on, I allowed anyone and everyone to participate in the planning meetings. I found out that *"not everyone"* is a good leadership participator. Be careful that you have selected the right people to be on your strategic planning team. After prayer, select people whom you feel led by God to invite.

Keep expanding the vision of the *"outpost ministry."* Include future attendees in your viewpoint. Dream a little. Help everyone concerned… to see that we are sprouting God's plan. Strategic planning will help you in creating a growth model. As I stated above, plan in advance to build, split into another group, and then split again. When you do the math, that's eight more jams created, all spreading the gospel through bluegrass gospel music.

John 14: 27

Peace I leave with you; my peace I give you. I do not give to you as the world gives. Do not let your hearts be troubled and do not be afraid.

1 Peter 5: 6-7

Humble yourselves, therefore, under God's mighty hand, that he may lift you up in due time. Cast all your anxiety on him because he cares for you.

Instrument Workshops

One great idea is to offer instrument workshops an hour before the Jam officially starts. Notice I used the term, *"Workshops"* rather than *"Lessons."* I found that *"Workshops"* encourage more participation. Experiment for a while and then develop the best consistent pattern for your locale. Encourage and solicit the existing Jam musicians to lead the instrument workshops. Participation in any form makes a Jam successful. Musicians love to play. They will usually become a workshop host if you ask. Prayer makes a huge difference in results obtained.

We have recently included "Voice Workshops," which encourage singers. Also volunteered are "Microphone Secrets," "Songwriting Basics," "Gospel Finger Picking," "General Guitar," "Intermediate Guitar," and "Claw-Hammer Banjo." Recently we have had requests for mandolin, autoharp, dobro, and fiddle workshops. Be flexible with the musician talents that surface. Continue to remember to ask. You will be pleasantly surprised. God will help you find the hosts and students.

Starting On Time?

At first, no matter what the starting time was… musicians and spectators simply didn't want to be the first persons to show up. In general, even now, the musicians never seem want to start on time. I think it's *"modern cultural crowd psychology."* Over time, I found that strictly adhering to a specific starting time didn't work very well. Even so, I was always glad to see more and more musicians drift in. As a very basic value, even though I prided myself about *"starting on time,"* musicians still just drifted in late.

Elizabeth, one of the early supporters and musician participants in the Jams, had a boyfriend who always caused Elizabeth to arrive late. This situation simply made it difficult to organize, do sound checks, and preparation. One time, I allowed my frustration to surface at an event at a mountain church. I regretted my words as soon as I spoke. I said, *"If you guys can't come on time, then just don't come."*

In the subsequent weeks, I invited Elizabeth for coffee. At the restaurant she informed me that my words had really hurt her feelings. She told me that her boyfriend was always late to everything. Even though she was an excellent *"play-the-piano-by-ear person,"* a guitarist, a singer, and a songwriter, Elizabeth was a passive personality.

I told her that, *"From now on, you will never have to worry about starting times."*

I modified my starting time philosophy to using the word, "*Approximately.*" I gave up trying to start on time. "*Approximately*" has made my life easier and much more peaceful. Surprisingly now, I have musicians consistently showing up early... how interesting?

Sound Equipment

To begin, invest in a microphone, amplifier, microphone stand, and a couple of music stands. Having the ability to sing into a microphone attracts musicians. I have found that, when a microphone is there, with just a little encouragement, musicians will come up and play and sing. We currently have expanded the Jams to accommodate the soaring volume of new musicians and spectators. We now use four microphones and a four-channel mixer board. We have also added feedback floor monitors.

Master Songbooks Draw Audience And Musicians Together

Create a master three-ring notebook: "*Gospel Jam Start Up Songs.*" Select 100 or more public domain songs (with chords).

Place the songs and index in *"one-inch"* three-ring binders. As I previously stated, we have changed from offering songbooks for free to charging a small amount to cover costs and provide a small profit. New attendee musicians will usually want to purchase the songbooks to take home and practice. The songbooks can be used to pass around during the Jam to the audience for singing along and making audience song requests.

Use the Internet to find songs with lyrics and chords. Format the songs so the songs print on one single page. In numerical order, hand-number each of the songs. To organize the song index, create a table in Microsoft Word or in an Excel spreadsheet. Use the sort function to organize the song titles alphabetically. Each time a new song is added, a new song receives the next highest number. Resort the list alphabetically, and reprint the song index.

For durability, I personally place each song in a plastic cover. My master three-ring songbook endures over time. When the musicians have a new song to play, I encourage the musicians to bring ten song copies (3-hole-punched). We have just begun requesting that songs be first submitted and approved by our Leadership Guidance Team. We want to keep our focus on gospel songs. These songs can be either the musician's own compositions or songs that might be new to the group. *Use your ingenuity.*

Egg Shakers

Always involve the audience. Purchase plastic egg shakers. Hand them out to the members in the audience who say they can't sing or play. Always acknowledge, and encourage the audience to join in. Passing out the egg shakers enhances audience participation. Always make the audience feel important and welcome. Thank people for coming. Continue to establish new friendships. Jams are fun. Ask the egg shakers!

Learning To Listen

If you pay attention, you will have plenty of opportunities to observe and listen. Most of my personal effectiveness comes from leaving the stage and mingling with the audience. "*Observing*" and "*Listening*" are two of the skills I have learned to do best.

For example, we had a big circle set up for one of the early jams. We were experimenting with a large circle concept rather than a horseshoe shaped setup. As we took turns choosing songs, I was on the outside of the circle. I heard whistling coming from a six-year old boy who had come with his grandpa and grandma. His whistling was clear and powerful as we played and sang, *"Amazing Grace."* I deftly moved one of the microphones over... closer to him. The emerging harmony was awesome.

At the end of the song, I asked everyone to play and sing the same song again. I asked that Brenden be given an opportunity to do a solo break, which he courageously performed and whistled on the spot. Because I listened, it was an inspiring miracle of encouragement happening.

Another Whistler

At an inaugural Jam I helped start with John Horner at the Senior Center building in Sterling, Colorado, I observed and mingled with the audience. An older gentleman was sitting in the front row of the audience. I heard his clear whistling tone above the singing. I went up front and told John, the leader, about the whistler. *"Oh yes, that's Bill. He is always whistling."* With my encouragement and John's urging, we got Bill to come up and join the musicians in the center. We had Bill take several solo-whistling breaks during the songs. In fact he enjoyed being with the musicians so much, he stayed the rest of the afternoon up front in his chair and took more solo whistling breaks.

Encouraging The Audience

Effective techniques have developed because of my encouraging people to come up and use whatever talents they might have. A Bluegrass Gospel Jam, in my opinion, is an innovative refreshing event that encourages folks to participate. We weren't all born as *"performers."* We weren't all born as *"participators."* However, I feel that *"we were all born with the capacity to encourage."*

I think I have a special talent to help utilize and motivate creativity. I think I have the talent to care for others. What would you do if you had opportunity? What does it take for you to generate a smile and one small step forward?

All it takes is one step of courage... courage to help someone else.

God can use you and me in ways contrary to what we think our own personalities might be. Can you whistle, shake an egg, choose a song, or encourage someone new, maybe even encourage yourself? Don't think you have any talent?

Surprise! Great! You're the type personality we can use at the Bluegrass Gospel Jams.

Break Times

Most important Jam time: *"Take a pre-planned break or breaks throughout the Jam."* Invite attendees to bring food and refreshments. Food and coffee create fellowship opportunities. The break times give folks time to go to the bathroom, get a cup of coffee, and to mingle with each other. The set-aside time also allows musicians to mingle with the audience. You will find you will receive many requests for songs during this time. I always try to honor each request as soon as we resume playing. This helps the audience to connect and take part in the jam. A pre-planned *"Break Time"* is a participation principle that works well.

Name Your Jam

I first chose the name, *"The Good Old Bluegrass Gospel Jam."* Feel free to use this name or to create your own. I suggest that the name you choose indicates that your group is a gospel group.

If you would like assistance in developing a personal gospel jam website, please let me know. ron@pursuitofpeace.net or www.bluegrassgospeljam.com

Preplanned Time Off

It's important that the head coordinator make set-aside personal time for him or her. Jams are no fun if they cause pressure, stress, or frustration for the leader. Always prepare to operate from a perspective of peace, serenity, and tranquility. An energetic leader makes all the difference. A peaceful energetic leader can lead in even better ways.

Segments Throughout The Year

I have the jams now in three segments during the year.

- Season 1: Sep, Oct, Nov, and Dec
- Season 2: Jan, Feb, March, April, May
- Season 3: June, July, and August

    (Change when needed)

At first, I did not schedule regular jams during June, July, and August. I took time off to go fishing. However, summers were still reserved for special occasion jams. No matter which month I chose to be off, I discovered that musicians still desired to have a place where they could gather and play. As the jam momentum increased, I found that there were plenty of musicians who would come to the summer jams. Along with other events that we get invited to attend, I now schedule regular summer Jams. We often get invited to play at outdoor summer picnic outings.

If I'm on a fishing trip, I ask someone else to substitute host the jam for me. When you allow helpers to assist, the jams still grow and expand. Jams are *"self-propagating."* Year-round jams are now our primary focus. *"I still go fishing with my grandkids during the summer."* I again encourage you to do your planning one year in advance.

Grand Finale Events

At the end of each season, I schedule a Grand Finale event. Hopefully your choice of location will be capable of having room for extra people. Email the entire gospel jam list, seeking participation. In addition, individually email each musician and ask if they would be interested in doing a special song at the Grand Finale. Sometimes, a reticent spectator volunteers to do a song simply because of being asked. There's usually a lot of reluctant talent silently residing within the audience members. Your mission is to illuminate and uncover those sleeping talents. Each time there is a response, add that name to the performer list, and email out that announcement to your email group. You will probably be surprised at who steps forward. A personal invitation is a powerful piece of gospel jam fishing tackle.

Using email, Facebook, and Craig's List, and press releases, start advertising the Grand Finale Gospel Jam event at least two weeks in advance. *Use any electronic media available.* Remember to make each email unique, but still include the original invitation. Again, encourage folks to forward the invitations to people they know who might come. Videotape your Jam. Place segments on *"You Tube."* Place the *"You Tube"* link into your email communications and onto your website. Use your imagination.

"Thank You" Emails

"Send out Thank You follow-up emails after every Grand Finale Event." Personally thank every performer for coming and participating. This extra amount of contact makes everyone feel important. The jam is not just about music. It's all about the people. People are investing their time in you and the jam. Word-of-mouth advertising works the best. A smile or two seals the deal. A *"Thank You"* pays huge dividends.

A Movement

The Bluegrass Gospel Jam Network is not an organization... *"We are a movement."* Why not become an active partner is this unique God-inspired movement? It's fun, rewarding, and important. What is your mission in life? What could your mission become?

Faith Steps

Each gospel jam is a series of faith steps. A leader has to believe in what he is doing. A good leader encourages others all along the path.

Proverbs 20: 24

A man's steps are directed by the Lord. How then can anyone understand his own way?

John 14: 33

I have told you these things, so that in me you may have peace. In this world you will have trouble. But take heart! I have overcome the world.

Isaiah 26: 3

You will keep in perfect peace him whose mind is steadfast, because he trusts in you. Trust in the Lord forever, for the Lord, the Lord, is the rock eternal.

Chapter 8 - Grow A Bluegrass Gospel Jam

Seven Stress-free Steps

1. Write down and make a list of your reasons why you want to start a Bluegrass Gospel Jam

- Put into writing your core values
- Find and write down the Bible verses that demonstrate your belief
- Find a location: Truck Stop, Church, Restaurant (the best locations are where food, bathrooms, and parking are readily available)
- Locate a sound system (four-microphone system works the best)
- Make a poster and put it up in strategic places (Utilize tear-off slips with phone number and contact person)

2. Determine the best days and times for you to host your Jam (once a month, or every other week, recommended)

- Plan your schedule one year in advance
- Leave room in the schedule for special invitations that come your way

3. Invite

- By word-of-mouth, personally invite musicians (of all skill levels)
- Utilize email, Internet, social media contacts, etc. Talk to friends.

4. Create a master songbook with words and chords

- (Plan to make songbooks available to musicians and audience)

5. As soon as possible, locate another encourager person to come alongside you

6. Purchase a "Gospel Jam Start Up Kit"

- Available at bluegrassgospeljam.com

7. Pray and Start!

Chapter 9 - Cultivate An Outreach

Phenomenal Growth

The Gospel Jams are now emerging into a second predominant phase of growth. Were there any concepts that changed? The answer is, *"Yes."* When did the growth spurt start? (That's a hard tongue twister to say!)

Karin, a real estate agent, one of the drop-in audience attendees, came up to me after one of the early jams and said, *"I want to be a sponsor. How much does it cost?"* Can you believe that I wasn't really prepared to answer that specific question? She was asking me how she could become a Bluegrass Gospel Jam Sponsor! All I did was place a sentence in the program brochure that stated, *"If you would like to become a Bluegrass Gospel Jam Sponsor, please contact me."*

That following week, Karin and I met for coffee at a Perkins Restaurant. Through exploratory conversation, Karin offered to provide new printed color brochures. I created the text and wording. Karin provided the formatting and color presentation. This newly fashioned classy program brochure advertised Karin's real estate business and has helped initiate even more interest in the Gospel Jams.

Gospel Jam Program Brochure

Here are portions of the text.

Thank you for coming!

I believe God invented music. The Bluegrass Gospel Jams were created to provide a wholesome family fun activity. We encourage both young and old talents in a welcoming environment. You and your friends are invited. Sometimes you become aware of talents you didn't even know you had. Sometimes your talents have been stored away in a closet. I am also in the process of developing the National Bluegrass Gospel Jam Network. Home based in Fort Collins, Colorado, we encourage the formation of local gospel jams in the surrounding communities. We are now beginning to expand into other states. My goal is to help spread the gospel all across the USA.

If you wish to learn how to play an instrument, the Bluegrass Gospel Jam is your place. All musicians started somewhere. Come and join in. I believe that God's work gets done through the music and the words of the songs we play. I know that's why we get together.

Propaganda Ron

Word of mouth advertising has continued to help the Gospel Jam grow. In addition, because of my consistent email contact, as one musician named me, I have now become known as, *"Propaganda Ron."* I count this description as a tremendous compliment. The email roster continues to steadily increase in number. At the Jams, I now announce to everyone, *"Do not sign up for the email notifications if you don't want to receive a lot of emails."* I received one request that stated, *"You were right. I have never seen so many emails come from one single source. Please remove my name from your roster."*

This just means the Gospel Jam messages are being seen, over and over. My email advertising is working. By the way, if someone wants to opt out from the email roster, I immediately remove his or her name. I only do *"permission-based"* email contact.

Memories

The years of Bluegrass Gospel Jams continue to be packed with special memories. We now post pictures and videos from the Jams. What does it take for you to create a special peaceful memory?

Psalm 60: 16
But I will sing of your strength, in the morning I will sing of your love;
for you are my fortress, my refuge in times of trouble.

God Guided Action

"Trusting in God brings in the people." My feeling is that divine leadership skills mature by trusting in God. *"Faith is God-guided action."* The Bluegrass Gospel Jam Trail is a path wizened all along the way with victories. Do you often travel the victory trail?

I have observed that many folks, whether young, middle aged, or old, rush around a lot. *"Keep busy,"* seems to be everyone's current mission in life. On the other side of this feverish *"rush-around era"* are the folks who always worry. Activities that are peaceful, calm, and valuable, are squeezed out of the happiness plan. It's all too easy for folks to ignore daily and weekly joy. It's all too easy to inhabit and repeat the same non-productive routine or pattern. It's all too easy to allow TV to determine your *"young branch existence."*

Do you allow *"anti-joy"* thoughts to interfere with peaceful planning? *Are you too busy... to participate in happiness?* Are you too full of activity?

Peaceful Pause

In the welcoming environment that the jams provide, we help people slow down for a tremendously peaceful pause. Attending a gospel jam is one of the best ways to relax, have fun, and meet other good people. Why are gospel jams peace producing? The reason is, *"We are singing about God, to God, and for God."*

It is important to note that the Gospel Jam is not altogether about the leader or the performers in the band. As I stated before, a Jam is a *respite spot for tired travelers,* whom I call, *"rush-arounders."* Are you one of those who are always in a hurry with *"schedules to keep before you sleep?"*

A Jam is a gathering house where the batteries of our souls get recharged. A Jam is where someone can come and be encouraged. It has become a blessing place for the musicians.

Psalm 39: 6

Man is a mere phantom as he goes to and fro: He bustles about, but only in vain; he heaps up wealth, not knowing who will get it.

Spreading Good Will

Are you *"jam-packed with life?"* Why not make music a dynamic ingredient in your life?

"You don't have time?" That's the most common phrase people use. Why is it so hard for folks to change a harried habit? Maybe *they* need to experience a Gospel Jam. Maybe *you* need to create a place where you can come and hear the gospel through the music the Jammers play and sing. The Gospel Jams *spread good will.* You are invited to help. Maybe all you have to do is to invite someone else. Maybe all you have to do is to encourage someone to invite *his or her* friends. You are welcome to become a catalyst for expansion and fulfilling a mission.

Romans 15: 13

May the God of hope fill you with all joy and peace, as you trust in him, so that you may overflow with hope by the power of the Holy Spirit.

People Will Respond When Invited

Over the years, I have found that most people are afraid to openly witness to others about God. Many searching souls are out there. These reticent searching souls are yearning for an invitation, from me, or from you, from someone.

Have you invited someone lately, to come and hear about God through music?

Can you envision yourself inviting somebody to come to a Gospel Jam?

Even if people don't come, they still appreciate the fact that you cared enough about them to make the invitation. "*Go and tell others,*" is a command in the Bible. The same is true of the Gospel Jams. Let God work his way. All you and I have to do is to keep on inviting and planting the invitation seeds.

I have also uncovered this observable and conspicuous truth: *People will respond when invited!* Can you find some innovative ways to help grow the Gospel Jams? Sure! How about finding the time to send to a musician, or to the leader, a *"thank you"* card, or even a *"thank you"* email? For me, these *"thank you"* comments are *always* a source of encouragement. The Bluegrass Gospel Jams continue to operate from a thankful and peaceful perspective.

Upbeat Encouragement

Whether in gigantic fashion or petite style, I sure appreciate everyone who participates in the Gospel Jams. I enjoy receiving complimentary emails, thank you notes, and all forms of appreciation. I need the encouragement "*pat-on-the-*

back" as much as everyone else. I rejoice when I have helped someone else. The whole resolve of the Gospel Jams is upbeat encouragement.

We have *"imprinted logo egg shakers"* that we pass out to the audiences. In addition to choosing songs, *"shaker eggs"* provide spectators with more opportunity to unite together. The *"egg-shaker-participation"* helps the Gospel Jams strengthen. Our volunteer musicians now write and perform new songs.

Learning And Accepting Environment

For clarification, the whole Gospel Jam encounter is not a *"rehearsed, over-and-over, pre-scheduled performance event."* First-timers are encouraged to learn as they go. Musicians fine-tune as they become better at their skills. This learning and accepting environment allows newer musicians to more quickly summon the courage to join in. The absolutely amazing result is that performance quality begins continually materializing and emerging from every participant.

1 Peter 5: 6-7

Humble yourselves, therefore, under God's mighty hand, that he may lift you up in due time. Cast all your anxiety on him because he cares for you.

"God Just Gave Me The Song"

We play and sing all types of gospel songs at the Jams. Some songs are pure bluegrass. Some songs have a country flavor. Countless songs come from old hymns. Many original songs, written entirely by the musicians, are emerging into the open. One Jam member wrote a song in the middle of the night during a stay at the hospital for food poisoning. *"God just gave me the song."*

Another Jam member drives home, pulls over on the side of the road, and writes a song. Then she calls everyone she can and sings the new song to them over the cell phone.

My daughter wrote her very first song during church, sitting on the pew. What is happening here?

Now isn't that amazing to see how God is working in others' lives? I believe the Holy Spirit is functioning and materializing right in front of our eyes.

Never Too Old Or Too Young To Learn

I have had to learn a lot about email, the computer, advertising, encouragement, thankfulness, delegation, problem solving, leadership, word selection, and even creativity. You may have a different set of skills that need to be developed and enhanced. I encourage you that you are never too old or too young to learn.

Knowing that God is actually leading me, keeps me going. How do I know? I feel his presence. I still read the Bible almost every day. I still turn over each day to him. I still get to see miracles happening in every day situations.

I received an email from Bryan. Shortly after starting up the original Bluegrass Gospel Jams, we put on an *"outpost outreach"* Jam at his church in Lyons, Colorado. This was our first experience at expanding into another community. This next week, Bryan is planning to bring his family up to a *"Home Jam"* at my house. He is a beginning banjo player. The Lyons outreach Jam was the first broad launch of the Bluegrass Gospel Jam *"Outpost Ministry." "Go out to the people."*

Our First "Away-From-Home Jam"

At Bryan's request, we did a Gospel Jam on a Sunday morning at his church in Lyons, Colorado, at a location that was an hour away from our home base in Fort Collins. Many of the Jam members told me that this event wouldn't work. The obvious reasons were, (1) *because of distance (an hour away)*, (2) *being Sunday morning*, (3) *because it had never been done before*.

To help out Bryan and his church, I did it anyway. I said, *"Yes,"* to his request, without consulting any of the Jam members. I didn't have any idea of what would transpire. I had some Bible verses marked in case no one showed up. Even though I am not a preacher, I mentally prepared to preach if no one from the Jam arrived on the scene.

"This Is What God Wants Me To Do"

The Lord blessed the event at Brian's *"Old Stone Church."* The church stage was jam-packed with musicians, both regulars and new local musicians. The church pews were full to capacity. At my encouragement, the entire audience joined in and sang along...the good old gospel songs.

A photographer took a picture of me up in the center of the stage behind the preacher podium. I think he captured me at the precise time I was feeling the spirit of the Lord telling me that, *"The Jam is good. It's doing God's work."*

I felt God with me. God's spirit flowed throughout the band members and the audience. I knew right then, *"This is what God wants me to do."*

Since that Sunday morning event, even though Bryan has been busy, he has been reading the consistent emails I send. I encourage you to never give up when you begin doing work for God. In other words, *keep on sending those emails*. You never know for sure what God's perfect timing is. Have courage and patience. God said he would never leave you nor give up on you.

Continual Guidance

As you draw closer to God, I'm sure you will also get opportunities to see miracles actually happening in the real world. *Peace*, through God, *opens the eyes of those who are too busy to observe*. If you search for the magnificence, there is a picturesque world out there. Why not take an undisturbed look around? I enjoy being on God's team. I believe I get continual guidance from God.

Occasionally, I have people problems, but these problems seem to dissipate over time. I am in the process of letting God handle the people problems. Now, I am in the process of solving the problems with prayer. It's sure a lot easier.

Overall, the Jams are moving forward with peaceful, joyful, and positive outcomes. I enjoy the challenge of helping people relax and find fun while participating and sharing in song. Playing an instrument is so much fun. I'm playing songs on the guitar I have never played before! How can that happen? Why not come to a Bluegrass Gospel Jam and find out?

The Jam truly is an awe-inspiring and marvelous encounter. We invite you. *"Come On Down to the Bluegrass Gospel Jam!"* This is the title of the opening song written by one of the Jam members. She is the one who pulls over on the side of the road and writes a song. God is working in *her* life.

At A Stoplight

I was in the left turn lane waiting for the signal to change. It was summer. My front window on the right was open. The person in the next lane on the right was saying something to me. *"I am an activity director. How much do you charge?"*

I replied, *"Nothing. We don't charge. We do everything on a donation basis."*

"I have your phone number off your back window. I will call and we can set something up."

"OK."

The arrow light turned green and I proceeded down the road. The next day, Pam called me and we set up a time to come and perform for a rehabilitation care center. At the end of the performance, she made a contribution of $50.00 to the Jam. The residents at the rehabilitation home immensely enjoyed the event.

Ecclesiastes 2: 10-11

I denied myself nothing my eyes desired; I refused my heart no pleasure. My heart took delight in all my work, and this was the reward for all my labor. Yet when I surveyed all that my hands had done and what I had toiled to achieve, everything was meaningless, a chasing after the wind; nothing was gained under the sun.

How To Find A Jam Near You

- Ask any musician if he or she knows where a jam might be happening this week or month.
- Search the Internet for jams in your local area.
- Email your own sphere of influence and ask questions.
- Someone usually knows someone else who plays music.
- Put up posters on bulletin boards and advertise that you are looking for a jam group.
- Ask at Guitar stores. You will be amazed at how many musician groups are happening already.
- www.bluegrassgospeljam.com

Psalm 37: 37

Consider the blameless, observe the upright; there is a future for the man of peace.

Garden Of Faith

"You don't have a Jam to go to?" Why not begin one? Why not encourage someone else to start a Jam you can attend. As I said, musicians are everywhere. Look around. Use word-of-mouth advertising. It's the best kind of advertisement. Be creative. It's as easy as locating a local gathering place. Can you become a one-person email coordinator? I did. Can you create and put up a poster? Can you invite? The people will come. Guaranteed!

Faith is like pushing the *"send"* or *"forward"* button on your email. If what you are emailing is valuable, the seeds of gospel music will germinate the spirit of the gospel and grow anew in a fresh garden. You will probably never know in advance, which people God wants you to contact. That's OK. God will help. If needed, why not let your imagination run a little wild?

Why not ask God to give you some glimpses of progress as you go? God will help the *"send"* or *"forward"* message travel to people you don't even know. *Faith is human courage in action.* How about saying a positive prayer just before you push *"send?"* Some day, someone will say, *"I came because my friend sent me this email... "* Wow, what a witness!

Please remember; I invite; God sends. My job is to welcome people in. Folks do have legitimate reasons and situations that develop. Be patient. The seeds of bountiful plenty have already been planted. The harvest abundance is coming soon. I can just feel it. I don't worry about the results. *You* don't have to worry about the results. I just keep on encouraging you, others, and even the sideline observers, to go out and make a positive difference in the world. Everyone can smile. Everyone can say, *"Thank you."* Everyone can help someone else. Can you extend an invitation?

God's Part And My Part

I practice patience. I encourage and invite. That's all that is in my control. I submit to God's planning and action steps. If I have done my part (the inviting and encouraging), then I don't have to worry about the results. Results are God's part. You and I can invite people. God will take the situation from there. As you go, God will illuminate your mind with inspired positive enthusiasm.

How can God work his miracles if his workers are too few? God can do it all, but don't you think God wants you and me to benefit, learn, and experience the joy of giving to others and helping others? Do you have faith? I didn't just sit down and dream up a goal of wanting to build a huge Gospel Jam network. That's the *"God's Part"* of the plan that continues evolving.

"Give And You Will Receive."

In the Bible, there is a very strange principle, at least strange to a lot of folks. The principle says, *"Give and you will receive."* Do I mean that success comes from giving first? Why sure! It's a Christian fact evidenced in every successful venture. What would happen if a business tried to succeed by offering poor service and *"greedy concepts"* of customer care. The business will go into oblivion very quickly.

I'm sure that creative ideas are buried somewhere inside of you. You may not be the individual Gospel Jam leader. You may have no musical ability (by the way, everyone uses that excuse for not participating.) God created you. *You* are important to God. You have probably just pretended to be unimportant to anyone.

Isn't there a spark of something in your heart that could help enlighten someone else's path, a gospel trail to follow? Don't you think God will send you the people and resources you need to carry on God's work? He does for me. I encourage you to seek out that person you are, and can be, in God. Just knock. He's always there, waiting for you to come in and pay a quick visit.

How Does The Gospel Jam Grow?

"I had to step out on faith first."

God supplies the people who should come. When you are trusting God to lead the way, God provides the miracle of growth. Gospel Jam growth is like a seed sprouting in the springtime. You plant and cultivate the seed early. When is *"early?"*

"Now" is the best time.

God always attends and oversees the Bluegrass Gospel Jams. I helped plan it that way. You can, too…

Psalm 40: 3

He put a new song in my mouth, a hymn of praise to our God.

Many will see and fear and put their trust in the Lord.

Chapter 10 - Wisdom Insights

Create Your "Purpose Statement"

Mine: *"Help others discover and apply principles of true peace"*

Create Your "Mission Statement"

Mine: *"Through encouragement, bluegrass gospel music, and Pursuit of Peace books, help men, women, and young people find true peace with God."*

Create Your "Vision Statement"

Mine: *"Thousands of people living fulfilled lives of true peace."*

Find A Friend Who Believes In You

Once-a-week coffee time with a down-to-earth friend will help guide you and focus your actions. A mission is no fun if you have no one with whom to share it. Each of you can be a spiritual mentor to the other. Sharing victories should be a common goal. Problems will have less power over you when you have good input and good insight from a good friend. Wisdom comes from experience, prayer, and creative consultation. Wisdom comes from a friend who is a bottom-line personality who can keep you on track. Sometimes, conversation is all you need. As you progress, you can invite a third person in to help contribute. *"A triple braided cord is not easily broken."*

Servant

As a Jam leader, you are a full-fledged servant. You provide the location and the strategy structure to *"welcome in musicians and spectators."* A Bluegrass Gospel Jam is an *"uncomplicated idea put into action."* The Jam materializes into existence because of one central idea, *"Let's all gather together and make music together."* The more you care for others, the more you are effectual in sharing the gospel.

Songs often bring out special treasured memories. Sometimes, one song can make a huge difference for one or more of the persons in the audience. Sometimes another musician on your left or right gets especially blessed. You never know what difference you can make in someone's life by offering respite peace and comfort through the special words of a song. God's word never returns void. Words in a song serve a purpose. All you and I have to do is choose and sing a gospel song. The song will reach somebody…

Give Credit To God

In everyday conversation, practice using words that are encouraging and positive. If needed, develop more optimism as a choice to live more fruitfully. A child doesn't learn to walk or talk until he is encouraged to do so. A child will absorb the attitudes and feelings he is exposed to and listening to.

The gospel jams are built with optimistic encouragement being the cornerstone of the foundation that is being laid. If we have shining performers who are perfect in performance, that's OK, as long as they don't get *"puffed up"* and overly concerned about personal performance. If a performer gets upset every time a mistake is made, then they just missed out on a blessing that can be shared with others. *"God wants us to go out and tell others."* He didn't instruct us to be perfect in all ways, all of the time. He just wants us to be concerned with our fellow man.

"Better to glorify God than to glorify one's self."

Reinforcing Desire To Learn

Musicians need continual edification. At least for me, learning to play an instrument, or to sing, takes a tremendous effort. Granted, some folks were born with a singing voice or an aptitude to play an instrument. If you are like me, most of us *"regular people"* have had to develop a desire to learn and a discipline to go along with it. And yes, one most important part is to practice. Jams are all about practice. Learning accelerates at the Jams. A compliment given to a musician can go a long way towards reinforcing that musician's courage and diligence. A negative comment can hinder or even halt progress.

I was trying to learn how to sing by standing next to a musician who was pretty much a performer leader. I was trying to emulate the finger positions on his guitar and was attempting to sing along with him. He turned and gave me the *"dirtiest look."* He was not seeking to help *me* along. I was spoiling his song performance. I retreated to the outer rim of the circle jam, where I became more inconspicuous. This experience was a setback for me and hampered my learning for a long time. My *"just-beginning courage"* quickly dissipated simply because of that *"dirty look."* That *"look"* caused me not to want to learn to sing and play. It was a major setback for me, an attempting musician.

First Time Singing Into A Microphone

Eventually, along with the other musicians, I started singing into a microphone. This was a true miracle from God. I don't know how to sing. I just do it. I pretend that I am singing for the Lord, and to the Lord, and I give it all I have. Miraculously my voice blends in with the other singers. I'm still learning. After all, it has taken 71 years to get to where I am now.

In one of the earliest gatherings, in a Sunday night church service, I had invited a piano player and a few young singers to accompany me on my singing debut. This was the first time for me to sing into a microphone in front of a bunch of people.

I stood center-stage, trying to sing my first public solo song (I was 61 years old.) In the middle of the song, I accidentally knocked over the microphone with the neck of my guitar. I was so intent on singing into the microphone that I followed the microphone down to the floor, still strumming and singing. It was totally embarrassing and funny at the same time. *"I was singing downward into the microphone sprawled out on the floor!"*

Kelli, the piano player, asked me *"if I wanted to pick up in the middle of the song where we left off?"* I said, *"No way!"* After returning the microphone stand to an upright position, we started over from the beginning. We were playing and singing, *"I Saw The Light."* Somehow I made it through the song. Now, that is courage! When I sat down in the front pew, I felt like a hot limp spaghetti noodle.

Bottom line... the Bluegrass Gospel Jams reinforce the desire to learn. If I can, you can. Have you ever garnered the courage to *"try?"* Or have you used that uncompromising phrase, *"I can't do that!"* I do a lot of things that I couldn't do before. What is your inner desire? What would you like to accomplish?

Seeking Help

At this time, I must admit that *"seeking help"* is one of my weakest areas. I am not very patient with folks who do not catch on to the same vision I have for the Jams. Even though my delegation skills are steadily developing and improving, my impatience sometimes causes me to attempt to take care of all the details all by myself.

I find myself thinking, *"It's easier to do it, myself."* This is a foolish way to go. Sooner or later, the little tasks build up and begin making the leader ineffective. Deliberately plan on asking for help and pray for the help to come. That's a much wiser plan.

Please remember you don't have to be a perfect leader before you become a leader. Just continue to learn as you go. Don't be afraid to seek help.

Choosing Helpers Wisely

I have a saying, *"Who do I let in my boat?"* This is a fisherman phrase I use to remind myself to exclude people who drag my spirit down. These *"drag-down"* people are not positive or supportive. When choosing leaders to be on your team, please realize that one negative personality can infect the attitude of the entire group. Selecting leaders and helpers requires a definite basic agreement with your vision for the gospel jams. There is no advantage to having a person on the team who doesn't understand what is trying to be accomplished.

Have leadership meetings by invitation or request only. Always be open to new joiners, but be prepared to explain to the new joiner what the guidelines are. Agreements in principle and vision are crucial to constructive outcomes. Be selective when choosing leaders and helpers. I have found there is no advantage to taking misguided detours in thinking. Constructive critique is fine.

I have found, however, that when someone *is given the opportunity* to participate in even the most menial way, they do become an active element of the gospel jam outreach ministry team. My job is to solicit and suggest opportunity. Delegation and better leadership skills are areas of improvement I need. I'm asking for more help from God… and others.

Not All Your Supporters Will Stay True

Musicians are artists. Each musician has a developed skill that has evolved through practice over the years. As a result of that polished skill, they can become very protective of their thoughts and opinions as to how things should be done. Also, please realize that a volunteer in your group might not be as dependent upon God as you are. His or her faith might not be the same as the *"outcome-thinking-faith"* that I encourage you to have.

Realize that there will probably develop over time, a rift of disagreement. In my experience, disagreement is a basic principle of group gatherings. Your job as a leader is to be aware of the inevitable rifts that can develop over even the smallest dissent.

Opinions have tremendous power over group dynamics. Be ready to adjust. Be ready to rise above the problems. These *"problems"* are usually opportunities to make the course corrections that God is suggesting you take. It isn't the end of growth. It's just a correction in the path, a curve in the trail, to get to where God wants you to be. It's a superior idea to pray first before choosing the leaders.

Monkey Wrench Throwers

Unfortunately, all groups have *"monkey wrench throwers."* These are people who will try to overly exercise their opinions, or who simply enjoy tearing down something good. Just watch out for them. They hide in the background gossiping and causing dissension. Just expect it, and rise above it. A Bluegrass Gospel Jam is a good thing. The devil doesn't want you or me to be fulfilled with doing God's gracious work. Just be on the alert, and take quick counsel of God's guidance.

Handling Miscommunications

A leader has to always be on the alert for both verbal and written miscommunications. Musicians are artists and can have their feelings hurt very easily. The artists have usually earned the right to be a performer. Many times I have taken the time to sit down over coffee with the individual who has been hurt. Once discussed and explained how there is always some discord between performers and beginners, the offended person has a better understanding. These coffee appointments have been one my most effective recruiting tools. Taking time to build relationships is the most valuable experience you can build upon.

Bad Days

Bad days come and go. Usher out the bad days as soon as possible. Bad days are part of life and always arise from the weak areas in your life. Invite good thoughts to come to you by sending out good vibes on purpose to the people you are serving. Bad days will start dissipating far more often. Good days will appear more frequently. *"Good"* days will become *"daily"* days.

Recommended Steps For Solving People Problems:

- Hear out the complaint.
- Take the information into consideration and process it through peaceful thinking time.
- Pray
- Then make a decision to adjust to, or ignore the complaint.

Don't be surprised when the *"performer artists"* begin complaining and criticizing about how the jam should be conducted. At first, being inexperienced as a leader, I tried to accommodate every complaint. This was a foolish action upon my part. Sometimes, I would have to say, *"The leadership position is always open for anyone who wants to volunteer."* I didn't have any takers. I found that it takes some time to develop and guide a team.

Regardless of the type criticism (just and unjust) you may receive, stay true to your own principles and guidelines. When your guidelines are clearly defined and explained, prayers are your best solution. God will see you through when you ask for and rely upon God's guidance. God will help you become a good leader. God will help you become a music and peace ambassador for him.

Walking By Faith

From the beginning, a Bluegrass Gospel Jam is a walk of faith. Fear will start dissipating in direct proportion to your faith. Welcome fear. It will be your biggest challenge and your biggest victory. From start to finish, *"overcoming fear"* is what it's all about. *"Walking By Faith"* is the shortcut to true success.

The Debate - Amplified Or Acoustic?

In small circle jams, several musicians gather and take turns choosing and playing songs. Most of the circle jams are acoustic. Most of the gospel jams we do… are audience participation jams in locations that will accommodate spectators. We allow the audience to participate. We use four microphones so that the music gets heard over the hubbub of conversation. We allow both acoustic and amplified instruments. This decision can go against *"purist"* bluegrass musicians who prefer to only allow acoustic music. This is an *"OK"* situation with me.

I have found that in larger settings, the amplified instruments accentuate the acoustic musicians, as long as the amplified musicians are controlled to keep the music tuned down to blend in. In fact, the audiences enjoy the music more when they can hear it. Acoustic music by itself has a hard time reaching the ears of a large audience in a packed room.

Training the musicians to work in harmony with one another is always a challenge. The leader should lead with a firm hand. Since I was new to music, I had to learn all these nuances by trial and error. God's words still permeate through the songs and efforts of all the musicians and singers. Controlled guidance by the leader keeps the Jam on course, whether acoustic, amplified, or both.

Psalm 37: 37

Consider the blameless, observe the upright; there is a future for the man of peace.

Another Debate - Secular Music Versus Gospel Music

Here are portions of a complaint email I received and answered back. It points out different viewpoints on what should occur during a Bluegrass Gospel Jam.

"Ron, missed you at Pierce yesterday. It was a good jam, very crowded, I almost left before it started but ran into Brad and Carina on the way out, whom I invited at church that morning. It's funny how God works sometimes. The last hour was basically country music. I have nothing against most country music. I sing it every Wed at the Wasatch Senior Center. However, it reminded me of the jam at the Harmony Church. Key word, Church. Secular music doesn't belong in God's house. Towards the end some folks ran out of Gospel songs. Since you are the leader, would you talk to the Pastor to say something about his church being the house of God and this is just a Gospel jam to praise the Lord? I would hate for this to turn out like the jams in Nunn and Pierce, which is OK for them, No churches being used there. He may lose a couple of musicians but he will keep a few too. Thank You. Brad"

My Response

Hi Brad,

I appreciate your input on the Jams. We do need a word of explanation here. From the very beginning, the Pierce Jam has never been an official "Bluegrass Gospel Jam." Several years ago, the person organizing the Jam actually did not want any connection with the "Bluegrass Gospel Jam." She wanted it to be completely separate. However, when I started going to Pierce, so I could improve my guitar playing skills, I noticed that the majority of the musicians there had originally attended the Gospel Jams. I did get to meet new musicians and invited them to our regular gospel jams. In fact a lot of those musicians are now regular participants. I do advertise the Pierce Jams because I have been asked. You will notice that I don't advertise them as a "Gospel Jam."

Contrary to your belief, I believe the Bluegrass Gospel Jams encourage participation from musicians who might never have been to a church before. They might not even be Christians. My goal is to attract those folks into a welcoming environment to rub shoulders with practicing Christians. The Bluegrass Gospel Jams are an "Outpost Ministry... with no walls." Yes, I do allow country and western songs if those songs get new musicians and spectators to participate and join in. I believe this is an extended part of praising the Lord. So I roll with the flow some with each person so that they continue to return and play and sing gospel songs. The Gospel Jams are not designed to be an internal clique of Christian musicians. In my opinion, we are not performers. We make it easy for someone to get involved with practical everyday Christianity. I love to see unsaved people come in because a musician they know has invited them to come. So... I respectfully disagree with your statement, "Secular music does not belong in God's house."

This is the hardest part of the Jams... to convince the musicians, both performer and participants, that this is a good way to invite people into church. I feel the same way towards beginner musicians of all age levels and experience. As I said, I do appreciate your input. I just needed to clarify for you what my goals and aspirations are for the Bluegrass Gospel Jams. I appreciate your understanding and I appreciate your concern. I enjoy getting feedback. Sometimes the Jam leadership gets very lonely. Maybe some day, we can get together for coffee, if you would like.

Thanks,

Ron

Reply from Brad:

Thank you and forgive me for being so narrow minded. You point is well taken and I believe you are right. Exposing all musicians to the Gospel is a good thing, especially when a testimony is given, I don't know what I was thinking, perhaps being selfish to only want to play Gospel. Thanks for your reply, it was well written and received, Coffee would be great. Brad

Finding Answers

- Pray first.
- Wait for the nudge to go forward.
- Take one step forward.
- Wait upon the Lord for the next step he is encouraging you to take.

I have found that this four-step answer process is the wisest progress path one can learn to follow. At first, the path was very difficult for me to understand. I was first exposed to this answer approach when I attended a businessmen's bible study. I discovered that this step-by-step plan worked in every instance. In any attempt in life, this is truly a blueprint for success.

Bible Verse Blurbs Of Wisdom Marketing

Within my desire to stay in touch with the folks in my gospel jam email database, I discovered a powerful ministry. I send out daily *"Bible Verse Blurbs of Wisdom,"* one verse per day. I receive back positive responses every week and sometimes daily. I never know which person or persons that particular bible verse will affect. I believe I am God's messenger, helping distribute the words of God at the right time. *"Keeping in touch with a daily bible verse"* is my *"Personal Outpost Ministry."*

"Number One" Key Principle

The Bluegrass Gospel Jam number one key principle is, *"It's not my Jam. It is God's Jam."* Pray ahead of time for God to send the people God wants to come to the Jam. Welcome all who come. Invite them to join in. Smile. Encourage. Learn each name on purpose. Invite them back. Invite them to sign up on the email roster. Take time to build a relationship. Find out something about each musician and attendee. *Learn names on purpose.*

Sharing Personal Testimonies

When the musicians take turns choosing and playing different songs, there is usually a personal story behind each song selection. Often, musicians extemporaneously share testimonies. I allow testimonies. We don't try to make the Jams a specific *"church activity."* We cater to folks who might never have gone to church, or who have been hurt in the past by church people. We encourage fellowship with other Christians in whatever walk of life they may be in at this precise moment of opportunity. We never know to whom God is reaching out. We do know that we are helping God through the songs and music of the Bluegrass Gospel Jam. We enable sharing. Gathering together in spirit is a unique faith encouraging opportunity. Together, we create a positive performance participation that God can use.

Psalm 47: 6-7

Sing praises to God, sing praise; sing praise to our King, sing praises. For God is the King of all the earth; sing to him a psalm of praise.

The Words You Choose To Use

Always be aware that what you say, and what is communicated, are not always the same. What people hear is determined by what's going on their life at this particular time. Thinking through, and judiciously choosing which words to use, can make an enormous difference. The words you use may be the key to that person receiving the timely encouragement he or she needed. Positive results, from masterful word choices, massively outweigh all the negative distractions. You can recognize high-quality results by counting the smiles on people's faces.

Repetition is required in whatever pattern you choose. Two weeks before each Jam, I begin sending out invitations to come to the Jams. I use *"Email Header Marketing."* The entire content of my email message is packed into the subject line of the email. The majority of email recipients will only scan the email titles. Always encourage forwarding email messages to friends and family.

When musicians and attendees begin realizing that they can forward an invitation and become an emissary for God, they have gained another skill for attracting new people. I remind you again, "*email messages do not always get read.*" Have you taken the time to determine in advance what you want the outcome to be? Think before you speak, ponder before you write, and pray before you send your message. Sometimes it's wise to wait for one day before you push the *"Send"* button.

Grandkids CD

Because of the connections the jams were making with other performing groups, a lot of musical developments happened. One of the groups at the bluegrass gospel festivals was an *"acapella" (no instruments)* group of about thirteen singers. I remember Tim, the leader and organizer. He was a towering man with a cavernous, resonant, deep baritone voice. His group performed at many events and especially at the bluegrass gospel festivals.

My three youngest grandsons, Mark 13 (Alto/Bass), Matthew 10 (Tenor), and Michael 8 (Lead) also sang harmony at the bluegrass gospel festival events. My daughter, Ronda, connected up with Tim and asked him to help her develop a CD for the boys. They had to hurry to finish the CD because Mark's voice started rapidly changing. The amazing result is that we have a unique CD that recreates golden family memories. The first song on the CD was written by my daughter called, *"Singin' For The Lord."*

This is the first song my daughter has ever written. She also created all the song, piano, and instrument arranging for the CD. I helped with the physical packaging and reproduction of the CD. It was a new original family event recorded with a totally marvelous outcome. Just coming to the bluegrass gospel jams opened up the opportunity for creativity.

I encourage you to encourage Grandkid participation at all times. This is one of the first reasons I formed the Jams. Make room for the younger generation. Build a legacy for them. What kind of legacy are you planning to leave with your family? Can you create valued memories on purpose? Legacy lasts over many lifetimes.

I play my Grandsons' CD in my car. It's a memory we created as an offshoot of the Bluegrass Gospel Jams. We are the launch pad for creating memories…and we have just begun.

What kind of legacy are you planning to leave with your family? Can you create valued memories on purpose?

Hebrews 13: 1

Keep on loving each other as brothers. Do not forget to entertain strangers, for by so doing some people have entertained angels without knowing it.

Chapter 11 - Maintaining The Momentum

The First Jam

Smiling, my eyes surveyed my situation. On cue, my fingers found the guitar chords. I was the jam leader. I was standing in the midst of bluegrass musicians and singers. The old church choir pews had been recently removed, forming a wide, perfect stage. We had four microphones set up. Amazingly, surrounding me were over twenty-five musicians, playing and singing. The invited spectators were singing in chorus, the good old gospel songs. My dream, the *"Good Old Bluegrass Gospel Jam,"* had come into being. As I stood there with the microphone headset, with my guitar plugged into the church sound system, I reflected back, to how God had honored my petitions and requests in a way far beyond what I ever envisioned.

How To Create A Ministry

Without even trying to purposely create a ministry, I'm beginning to understand that the Bluegrass Gospel Jams have evolved into a real live ministry of peace, music, and participation. I believe God has orchestrated this unique situation. Bluegrass Gospel Jams, combined with my Pursuit Of Peace books, have made my life more exciting. My life is chocked-full of visible, tangible results. A few years ago, Mike, my music pastor friend, told me that, *"I was having an impact on people I didn't even know, yet."* That's the exciting part for me. I get a special thrill out of helping guide people I don't even know, closer towards God. Through books, through music, through participation, I believe God's spirit is reaching out and encouraging the musicians, the audiences, and even you, the reader.

Living Triumphantly

Is it possible that God can work more effectively, more completely, when we put our trust and faith in him? That's what is happening in my life right now. I live an amazing life, full of peace. I am growing stronger in faith every day and every week. Through *me*, God is helping me write his message of encouragement, to you, and to the friends to whom you pass on this book. Can life be lived triumphantly, most of the time? I say, *"Yes."* What do you say? I can only report the facts as they have unfolded over the years. If you want help with the thoughts and the God results, I will share with you, the concepts that have helped me become what I am becoming…a scribe for God and an ambassador for peace. I am on a mission.

A Wiser Goal Process

My assignment task is to help demonstrate to you and others that, when we follow God, there is joy, *"joy-unspeakable and full of glory."* In everything you and I do, God will allow us to achieve goals. God is infinitely much wiser than we are. Why not include a goal process that allows you to become what God has in store for you? The outcome will probably be better than you ever dreamed… Couldn't that idea of living a better, more peaceful life, possibly inhabit and reside in your mind? I'm talking of *"faith principles,"* studied, conceived, implemented, and shared with others. In short, I'm talking about living and experiencing a *"faith-guided life."*

Someone Has To Be The Leader

This is the embryonic phase. Yes, that person can be you. Perhaps you already consider yourself to be a leader. If you are like me, I never thought about being an organizer or the person in charge. Either way, we can each develop skills and become effective Bluegrass Gospel Jam leaders. The Bluegrass Gospel Jam *"at-large members"* are a loose group of volunteer musicians. Mostly, they just want to come and play. Most of the musicians just want to be included.

In my experiences, I have found that most don't want to participate in the implementation and planning details. At first, folks seemingly are always *"too busy."* Many are just followers. Be aware that this is a fairly normal reaction in just about any group. You, as the leader, have a continual challenge to bring in creativity and participation. I find myself praying more often. I have to continually have patience with God. He sends me the right individuals at the right time. I believe God has plans that I am not aware of as of yet. Once attendees start coming, my personal obligation is to encourage and invite them to return. I repeat often, *"Thanks for coming."*

Psalm 33: 1-3

Sing joyfully to the Lord, you righteous; it is fitting for the upright to praise him. Praise the Lord with the harp; make music to him on the ten-stringed lyre. Sing to him a new song; play skillfully, and shout for joy.

Introduce Yourself With A Smile And A Handshake

Remember Names *"On Purpose"*

"Hi, my name is Ron!"

If you make up your mind, in advance, to choose to remember, recall can be done. I smile and attempt to greet each and every attendee, both musician and spectator. "*On purpose*," I try to learn their name. I ask, *"Are you from around here?"* Then I listen intently to their response. I find out a lot of information by asking that one simple question.

When I meet them again, if I can remember their name a month or two later, I have instantaneously become a good friend. They feel when I am sincere and care about them. If a lot of time has passed by, it gets very difficult to remember the name. Sometimes I try to guess their name.

Another way to grab their name is to say, *"We've met before... haven't we? Help me with your name again."* I then deliberately spell their name out loud, which helps me to install the name in my own memory bank. This step takes courage and fortitude. Why not simply smile and admit, *"I have forgotten your name."* They probably don't remember yours either, even though you are the person in charge. Most of the time, they will respond with, "*I can't remember names, either.*" If you genuinely want to, *you can learn to remember names*. It's the best way to fire up and establish a good harmonious relationship.

Say "*Thanks*" often. Introduce each new musician personally to the other jam musicians. Shift over and make physical room for each new arriving musician. Always be, *"The Great Encourager."* It all starts and ends with learning someone's name.

Take Your Leadership Role Sincerely

Please realize that you are a diplomat for God. People will study your reactions. People will examine your motives. People will assess your way of thinking until they feel they can trust you. They will peruse your face for any signs of discouragement or unhappiness. They will pay attention to your real personality traits. They will come alongside you when you come alongside of them. What's the difference between a leader and the people in the audience? Nothing really. The leader just had the courage to step out first... and start.

Keep The Music Flowing

Be comfortable with being in charge. Keep the music flowing. No dead times when someone isn't prepared to take their turn at choosing a song.

Be Dependable And Tranquil

Always show up ahead of starting time. On the morning of the Jam, always remember to *"turn the whole Jam over to God."* Let God figure out which musicians and spectators are supposed to come. Practice knowing that, *"God is in control."*

Ephesians 5: 19-20

"Speak to one another with psalms, hymns and spiritual songs. Sing and make music in your heart to the Lord, always giving thanks to God the father for everything, in the name of our Lord Jesus Christ."

Be Thankful For The Musicians And Audience

Become a *"Thankful Encourager."* Build people up. Everyone needs the welcoming spirit of encouragement.

Be Willing To Learn

A Bluegrass Gospel Jam leader learns as he goes. Be OK with making personal mistakes. Be OK with others making mistakes. Smile inwardly and outwardly.

Magic Of The Jams

What happens when you gather a group of musicians together to play and sing? At first, a collection of confusion takes place. How does harmony emerge when everyone is playing at a different level of expertise? That's the magic of the jams. It's similar to sitting around a fireplace on a

Saturday night, sipping coffee, eating pie, and playing as a small group with four or five friends.

Hebrews 13 1-2

"Keep on loving each others as brothers. Do not forget to entertain strangers, for by so doing, some people have entertained angels without knowing it."

Expanding Too Fast

Early on, as the jam network began rapidly expanding, I began receiving requests for the Gospel Jam to go and perform at other cities in the Northern Colorado area. Our home base was located at a truck stop banquet room located in Johnstown, Colorado. I began scheduling Jams in other cities at other locations. I was amazed that so many musicians began showing up at the new locations. I found that, as soon as musicians found out about a jam, the musicians would drive from as far away as one and one-and-a-half hours distance. Over the early years, as the *"spreading out"* gathered momentum, I found myself being spread too thin. Even the travel back and forth started stretching my personal budget too far.

I enjoyed every moment of traveling to and playing in another location. However, I gradually lost control of the expansion. I expanded too fast, and spent too much of my own money, using credit cards, with no reimbursement. In addition, other musicians in the group started wanting to take over the controls of the jam network.

Even though I started up the jam network from scratch, I received a lot of untrue and unjust criticism. My feelings were hurt. Later, I began realizing that God wanted me to begin traveling a different road. I was trying to create a national system of gospel jams. I began realizing that God wanted me to slow down and concentrate on the local scene. I was in no position to manage a national effort. I still encourage the formation of bluegrass gospel jams all across the USA. I encourage, but now I don't try to personally manage a national network.

Why Musicians Love To Jam

Musicians love to play and sing. Musicians appreciate the philosophy of playing together as a group, especially with a group who has a mission. The Jams allow musicians to hone their skills, to make mistakes, and to improve. Musicians enjoy entertaining others. The Jams are magnets for attracting new musicians and spectators.

Ron's Three Rules:

1. *"Announce clearly the name of the song to both the musicians and the audience"*
2. *"Tell what key the song will be played in"*
3. *"You can't turn your back to the audience"*

Musicians Will Return

Musicians will tend to return to an environment where they are continually learning. Musicians will return when personally invited to return. The leader's job is to invite and encourage.

Become a Good Positive Communicator

Be positive. Establish guiding principles that you have prayed about and have taken the time to write down. Promote positive teamwork and camaraderie. Adopt a healthy calming communication style. Concentrate on setting the correct tone. While speaking, use appropriate emotions and tones. Think about the words you choose to use. In your private planning times, use the concept of *"outcome thinking."*

"What do you want the outcome to be?"

Always Involve The Audience

Be encouraging and welcoming. Purchase some plastic egg shakers. Pass out the egg shakers for the audience to use. Invite the audience members to come forward and help sing. Rely on God's nudges during the Jam…to decide whom you should individually encourage.

Make Sure You Are Understood And Heard

Repetition works wonders. There are always new participators and attendees. Speak closely into the microphone so everyone can hear. Utilize sound checks prior to starting the Jam. Adjust volumes during the Jam. Discourage *"musician chatter and plunking"* between songs. We call it *"noodling." "Noodling"* is very distracting. It's all too easy to lose the audience.

Courtesy Within

No matter who walks in the door, install and implement courtesy and acceptance. Sharing opportunities to participate helps the Jams mature, physically, spiritually, and emotionally.

Smile

Become an accomplished friendly and openhearted communicator. Be consistent. Intentionally visualize and fashion a Bluegrass Gospel Jam as a *"Fun Learning Place to Participate."*

Colossians 3: 16

Let the word of Christ dwell in you richly as you teach and admonish one another with all wisdom, and as you sing psalms, hymns and spiritual songs with gratitude in your hearts to God.

It's All About Everybody

Most people go to a musical event for entertainment. Then they go home and seek another event that will entertain them more. In short, as soon as the event is over, the event is forgotten. At the gospel jams, another feeling permeates and perseveres. Audiences leave after the jams are over, but they almost always exit with a very special desire to return, thinking about whom they can invite to come next time. When musicians catch the philosophy that their music does not have to be performed in a *"perfect performance"* manner, they begin catching the spirit that the Jams are a place to share and have fun while learning.

Rehearsing over and over to become a professional group is not our primary mission. Whether old, young, *"rusty,"* a beginner, or a performer, our mission is to encourage folks to try. Miraculous professional music does, however, continue to evolve. We offer the beginning platform. We are the *"catalyst of encouragement."*

1 Corinthians 15: 33

Do not be misled. Bad company corrupts good character.

Enlarging The Big Picture

My job is to encourage start-up leaders to look beyond the event and watch for results to start pouring out. It's easy to get bogged down with administration details and hiccups. From personal experience, I can assure you that it is never too late to ask God to show you the big picture of what you can do for God. He is waiting and watching for you to look towards heaven. I have even asked God to give me glimpses of outcomes as I go. Often, God gives me fresh insights.

For example, I receive an email back with a positive response. I receive a phone call from someone who wants to attend an instrument workshop. I receive a request from one of the attendees who gives me the email address of someone they want me to invite and add their name to the gospel jam roster.

I wear my Bluegrass Gospel Jam jacket to church. I enlarge the boundaries one conversation at a time. I place the Bluegrass Gospel Jam Logo and my phone number on my vehicle. At restaurants, grandkid basketball and baseball games, tennis matches, and public functions, I wear my Logo Bluegrass Gospel Jam jacket. Our blue denim shirts have the Bluegrass Gospel Jam logo embroidered above the pocket. We carry invitation post cards to pass out. We carry Bluegrass

Gospel Jam business cards. We are continually planting the mustard seeds of faith for expansion.

Scripture Foundation

Early on, I again encourage you to choose a basic bible verse that you wish to stand upon. Publish it for public view and stand firm on your conviction. Look inside your heart. Start reading the bible daily to help maintain your on-track walk with God. Walk by faith. Don't worry. If you pray that God will send you the people and resources you need, that's all you need. Be patient. Share your victories. Continually think about your victories. *"Your faith will lead you to wherever God wants you to be..."*

2 Corinthians 5:17

Therefore, if anyone is in Christ, he is a new creation; the old has gone, the new has come.

Spectator Perspective

What do the audiences want to see? They want to see musicians up front having fun sharing their music. Spectators want to feel good that they have come. Spectators want to sing along with the good old time-tested songs that have evolved and remained throughout the generations. When spectators are included, they feel like an integral part of the Jam. Music welcomes them in. Jam singers make the words of gospel songs come alive. We don't have *"dead audiences."* The audiences are *"live participants."* The leader's job is to provide that living spirit of bluegrass gospel music and musician participation. Spectators are *"advance scouts"* who invite new people to come.

Musician Perspective

What do musicians want to experience? Musicians want to feel appreciation, acceptance, and a sense of ongoing fulfillment. Camaraderie generates cooperation. Cooperation generates harmony. Harmony generates the Holy Spirit. The Holy Spirit makes a gospel jam extend and glow far beyond the end of the event. As a *"witness activity,"* there is nothing better for a musician to do than to tell a friend that he or she was out playing music all afternoon at a bluegrass gospel jam.

Word-Of-Mouth Referrals

As the leader, you need to encourage and remind folks to talk to their friends and family. Most folks don't seem to fully realize and appreciate the power of a personal invitation. Many have a habit of *"failing to invite."* Many folks don't think about others long enough... to generate a personal invitation. They don't practice *"inviting."* Many folks forget that they can make a positive difference in someone else's life just by being friendly. In short, they need to be reminded to reach out to someone else. I simply call it, *"thinking ahead."* Embrace and encourage the folks who are always inviting someone else. Word-of-mouth referrals make a jam grow faster than any other advertising or process.

People Will Respond When Invited

The leader's primary task is to step out, go forward, have fun, and invite and bring alongside as many folks as possible. *"People will respond when invited."* The leader needs to be the primary invitation extender and encourager. People will follow a good leader. Here is an email I just received this morning:

"Hi Ron,

Thank you for introducing me to the Bluegrass Gospel Jam. I think it is great. I felt very much at home there. The people were exceptionally welcoming. I had a wonderful time. I would like to continue going when I am able."

Managing God's Part

Don't even worry about it! God will not give up on you when you are working on doing God's will.

Isaiah 40
They that wait upon the Lord shall rise up as with wings of eagles. They shall run and not grow weary. They will walk and not be faint.

Managing the Musicians' Part

Don't even worry about it. Let the musicians grow. Be a true passion-filled role model they can trust and relate to.

Share The Victories

Share the gospel jam victories whenever you can. Take time to appreciate people. Nurturing occurs when you are serving others. Humility and openness connect all threads of communication.

Pictures And Videos Make Lifelong Memories

Take pictures at every Jam. Focus in on the faces as well as the group setting. Place pictures in your email messages. Review the photos to remind you of the good you are doing. Take videos of each jam event. Post the videos on *"You Tube"* and on your websites for future generations to view.

Develop Instrument Workshops

This activity will bring in more new folks than any other effort. Existing musicians will normally help if they are openly asked to do a workshop. But you do have to ask. That's your job as a leader. Simply ask your email roster what kind of instrument workshop they need. Then ask the musicians if they can supply that need. Match the needs and watch for positive results. A sixty-minute instrument workshop prior to the jam works wonders. Even the current musicians in your jam will participate in workshops so they can improve or learn a new skill.

The *"Break"* In The Middle

Taking time on purpose, for a fifteen-minute break two times during the jam, is the wisest and most important time investment a jam leader can make. The breaks allow musicians and audience to informally mingle and visit. Song requests often come during the break time.

121

Request in advance that audience members bring food and snacks for the *"break"* intermissions. Coffee, ice water, and food create an enveloping conversation atmosphere. Everyone gets the opportunity to get a drink of water, use the restroom, or to just stretch and walk around.

"Mingling Time" acts as a cohesive force that automatically and rapidly develops *"getting to know someone."* Have plenty of advertising items displayed. Have future schedule information that can be taken home. Always encourage folks to sign up on the email roster. This email roster provides the necessary essential contact information that keeps the jams growing.

Luke 12: 25-26

Who of you by worrying can add a single hour to his life? Since you cannot do this very little thing, why do you worry about the rest?

Websites And Blogs

Being of the older generation, I struggled with the concept of creating a website. I had two very good *"technical-oriented"* friends who encouraged me. I discovered that I had a true reason for putting up a website. My desire is to expand the formation and startups of new Bluegrass Gospel Jams all across the USA. I began to quickly learn web design concepts. The idea of a Blog that I could create by myself intrigued me.

Gradually I found that I could design a website using a Blog format. I found that operating and writing a Blog could be turned into a free website over which I had control. In other words, I could post writings and pictures and then make changes and updates when needed. The best part of this concept was that it was free. Inquiries come in steadily now, from all over the USA, Canada, England, and recently even one from South Africa. The Blog Website is growing nationwide and internationally. I recommend utilizing the website/blog combination as an effective communication tool. My website/blog is interactive.

We are in a changing society. We need continual updating capability. The free Blog Website is a better deal for me because I have learned to make my own changes and postings. Learning this skill took some time. I found out that other businesses needed my expertise and would even pay me for my *"newly-developed"* expertise. An income stream started flowing my way... just because I learned new current applicable information techniques.

I plan on offering very reasonable pricing for advertisers who support the Jam concepts. We will see what God wants to do with this concept.

We now post videos, have free music downloads, and downloadable E-books. We have just begun. We can let our imaginations run a little wild. In all my email communication, I have hyperlinks that take readers immediately to the Internet web pages where the readers can purchase both my hard cover books and my new E-books.

The bottom line... you can be creative, too. Electronic media advertising is a seed that has just begun to sprout. The results, when planted in good soil, will be a hundred times more fruitful. I just today sent an email press release to the local newspapers. This is just the beginning...

Bluegrass Gospel Festivals

Through word of mouth advertising and website/blog communication, I became acquainted with Suzie and her husband. They are musicians who make a living by performing musically for nursing homes, rehabilitation centers, regular bluegrass festivals, and other venues. Many years ago, Suzie came up with a simple idea, *"Wouldn't it be a neat idea if we had a whole festival that was entirely gospel music?"*

That idea has currently materialized into over thirteen years of Bluegrass Gospel Festivals over several states. Gospel musicians and family bands now sign up one year in advance to attend and perform. We, as a Bluegrass Gospel Jam group, have been invited to present workshops at the Colorado festivals on, *"How To Start A Bluegrass Gospel Jam."*

Suzie coordinates and encourages performer bands. Impromptu jams develop automatically at the festivals. These are what I call *"parking lot jams"* or *"RV Porch Jams."* Musicians sit in chairs by their RVs and start spontaneously jamming. *"Walk bys"* stop and join in. Gospel Jams and Bluegrass Gospel Festivals have a mutually beneficial symbiotic relationship. Both thrive upon reciprocal encouragement. We have a hyperlink to Suzie's website. Suzie has a hyperlink to the Bluegrass Gospel Jam website. We compliment each other.

Isaiah 26: 3-4

You will keep in perfect peace him whose mind is steadfast, because he trusts in you. Trust in the Lord forever, for the Lord, the Lord, is the rock eternal.

Chapter 12 - Seven Essential Principles

Seven Essential Mustard Seed Faith Principles

Matthew 17: 20

...I tell you the truth, if you have faith as small as a mustard seed, you can say to this mountain, 'Move from here to there' and it will move. Nothing will be impossible for you.

1. Outcome Thinking

Leading a gospel jam full of musicians is an indomitable task. Once you get started, as one musician put it, it is similar to *"herding cats."* Again, the question you need to ask yourself up front, and clearly define, is to ask, *"What do I want the outcome to be?"* What goals do you have for the Bluegrass Gospel Jam?

Worldly goal setting technique:

- Set a goal
- Project a finishing date
- Work hard and long

Spiritual goal setting technique:

- Pray
- Wait for guidance
- Take a step
- Wait for guidance
- Don't set a date
- Follow God's nudges
- Follow the path of creative inspiration
- Have faith in God
- Read the Bible
- Share with others

- Encourage others along the way
- Work happily as you go.
- Establish Balance
- Encompass Spiritual Perspective
- Take Faith Action Steps
- Watch For God-Guided Outcomes

I have experienced setting goals and achieving goals both the world way, and the spiritual way. *"It's my viewpoint that neither you nor I, as mortal human beings, are smart enough to figure out in advance where we should go."* I agree that people can set out a goal, work hard to achieve it; but if they end up being unhappy, why did they donate all their time working? Is making money an unfulfilled promise in your life? Do you have that hollow unfulfilled vacant feeling?

I believe that setting a goal utilizing God's counsel does just the reverse. Conceived by you and God, from beginning to end, you can work jointly towards achieving goals. Can you be satisfied with God leading you? Can you be happy living and genuinely believing in God's promises? Do you believe it's possible to end up at a better place than you could have arrived on your own? I've found God's way is superior to my way.

Matthew 11: 28

Come to me, all you who are weary and burdened, and I will give you rest. Take my yoke upon you and learn from me, for I am gentle and humble in heart, and you will find rest for your souls. For my yoke is easy and my burden is light.

The goal setting patterns are the same. The results are different. Wouldn't you want, when faced with a choice, to choose peace over strife? When I turn my life situations over to God, I don't have to worry about the outcomes. This is a marvelous experience of peace. I invite you to join in with me. *I encourage you to experience living the spiritual pattern of success and genuine fulfillment.*

The Gospel Jams are growing by faith and solid leadership principles (which I am in the process of learning more and more.) At the Gospel Jams, through fun and participation, we spread God's word through music. We are the *Jam*; we *spread* God's word. Gospel Jam victory stories are as real as hot buttered wheat toast, lightly browned, with sweet red strawberry jam on top for extra delicacy.

John 14: 7

Peace I leave with you; my peace I give you. I do not give to you as the world gives. Do not let your hearts be troubled and do not be afraid.

2 Thessalonians 3: 16

Now may the Lord of peace himself give you peace at all times and in every way…

Psalm 37: 37

Consider the blameless, observe the upright; there is a future for the man of peace.

2. Participation

Participation in any form is the key building block for establishing a Bluegrass Gospel Jam. The more you welcome in musicians and audiences, the more effect you have on the community in which you live. The Jams become their own sort of mini-community that spreads the gospel through the singing and the playing of gospel music. It's a center-of-attention gathering where new folks join in. It's a valued memory-making event that stirs emotions in hearts. It's an event that endures through many generations.

We involve everyone we can. We have a digital camera. I am beginning to solicit help by recruiting someone to be a Jam photographer to take pictures. The same is true of the digital video camera. I encourage and ask gospel jam attendees to distribute songbooks on the chairs. I ask someone to pass around the email sign up sheet. I ask other musicians to help me lead songs. I ask for help in having someone stand at the display table so they can help with sales of books, apparel, CDs, and *"Gospel Jam Start Up Songbooks."* I ask someone pass out the Gospel Jam flyers.

At first, I did all these tasks by myself. It is a much better idea to ask others for help. The participation principle has far more positive effects. When guests are welcomed and given an easy task to do, the stage is set for future harmonious relationships.

By allowing audiences to choose songs, everyone gets an opportunity to participate in the Jam gathering. Sometimes, when I sense it from God, I ask the person requesting the song, to come up front and join in with us up front. At first, they are almost always reluctant. I encourage them anyway. Once the person joins in, they return to their seat with a smile on their face. Often times I get other friends to come and join in with the one brave volunteer. Everyone smiles.

When possible, everyone gets to do something they have never experienced before. A Gospel Jam is a *"one-of-a-kind"* experience. If spectators say they can't sing or play, I pass out egg shakers so they can keep up the beat. "*A whole lot of 'shakin' goes on at the Gospel Jams.*" It actually works out better when I have a little boy or girl pass out the egg shakers. Again, I enjoy all of these tasks, but I still realize that I have an overall responsibility to lead, coordinate, and involve others whenever I can.

It's a large responsibility to be the overall coordinator. I tremendously enjoy the tasks. These collective tasks are the tidbits of wisdom that culminate in creating a welcoming thriving atmosphere. I just have to remember to let somebody in on the nuggets of wisdom. Participation makes everyone feel more comfortable. Every attendee is honored whenever possible. You can be creative and you can set the tone. Look for ways to involve everyone.

Psalm 37: 37

Consider the blameless, observe the upright; there is a future for the man of peace.

2 Thessalonians 3: 16

Now may the Lord of peace himself give you peace at all times and in every way...

Philippians 4: 7

And the peace of God, which transcends all understanding, will guard your hearts and your minds in Christ Jesus.

3. It's Never Too Late To Start

I started the Bluegrass Gospel Jams late in life. Here is what I wrote right after my double bypass heart surgery.

"If I could start out a new life, I want to be happy. I am choosing to remove all stress from my life. I want to be a kid again, and I will achieve that status through my kids, and grandkids. Every business thing I do will concentrate on getting the most out of every effort, in the least amount of time. I choose to gain more free time, all of the time. I am semi-retiring now, and enjoying my life now."

No matter what your age, God can use you. A Bluegrass Gospel Jam is an excellent way to reach folks with the gospel message. God will guide you from where you are to where he wants you to be. Pray, respond, take a step, and turn your whole new venture over to God. Just get started. *Musicians and audiences are just waiting for you to start.* It happened for me. I am thrilled that God uses me as one of his couriers. You, too, can become an ambassador.

Psalm 29: 11

The Lord gives strength to his people; the Lord blesses his people with peace.

John 14: 27

Peace I leave with you; my peace I give you. I do not give to you as the world gives. Do not let your hearts be troubled and do not be afraid.

4. Gospel Jam Etiquette

Printed Suggested Guidelines: Ron's Three Rules

1. Announce name of song
2. Announce what key in which the song will be played
3. You can't turn your back to audience

Be prepared to take your turn

If you are not ready, we will pass you by. No extra *"dead time"* between songs

Continual music

The chooser of the song shall direct the *"instrumental breaks"* about 5 words before chorus ends... Let instrumentalists shine... Back off by playing softly

If you get off beat or off key during a song, stop, listen, and then begin again

Encourage your fellow musician. Ask for help. Help him or her (in a nice friendly way)

Electrified instrument players, percussion instrument players, do not be offended if the leader asks that you turn down your volume. We are primarily an acoustic Jam. Do not seek to overpower the acoustic instruments

If you have a new song, please bring 10 copies (3 hole punched) with words and chords above the chord changes

Develop good interactions between you and the audience

Make physical room for musicians coming in

I welcome anyone to come and join in. Positive encouragement is the key element for both building relaxed camaraderie... and establishing enjoyable Jams.

Hebrews 13: 1

Do not forget to entertain strangers, for by so doing some people have entertained angels without knowing it.

5. Outpost Ministry

A Bluegrass Gospel Jam is an *"Outpost Ministry With No Walls."* We reach both believers and nonbelievers where they are. We take the Gospel music to the masses and have fun while communicating the message through music and participation. Camaraderie develops between musicians, singers, and audience.

We encourage the start-up of smaller performer groups who go out and share the gospel through music. New musicians and singers are welcomed and encouraged to try. We help shine up *"rusty musicians,"* who have, for a long time, left their instruments and talents gathering dust in a closet or garage.

Bluegrass Gospel Jams emerge as soon as a new location is announced and communicated. Performer musicians start coming from everywhere. The harmony is awesome. New songs begin emanating from the participants. Word-of-mouth and email invitations stir emotional and moving responses in people's hearts. We provide the opportunities for positive and rewarding contributions.

We turn *"I can't"* into *"I think I can."* We turn *"I think I can"* into *"I'm doing it."*

If you have reluctantly been holding back from participating, just be reminded that, *"These are God's Jams, not mine or yours."* When you participate, you are becoming an example for others to follow. When you comprehend that you are not being paid to do a performance, you get to feel first hand the awesome sensation of a music ministry simply created for others. The harmony that ensues is the magic and mystery of *"spreading the gospel."* Jesus told us, *"Go out and tell others the message of the gospel."* Guaranteed, someone else will be blessed by the efforts we use to share with others.

How long has it been since you and your friends and family sat around a fireplace in a family room and made music together? Have you taken time to slow down for fun? That's what we do at the Bluegrass Gospel Jams. No one falls asleep at the gospel jams.

We minister through fun, encouragement, and involvement. We pray and rely on God to send the people whom God wants to come. You can help at any time, through finances, through helping with administration details, to becoming a front-line greeter with a smile and a welcoming handshake. We want to learn your name, too.

And yes, we can demonstrate to you how to become the leader that you can be. *"Yes!"* All it takes is a small initial step of faith. Pray and take that first step.

"We welcome you. You have been invited!

Do you know someone you can invite to join in?"

John 14: 7

Peace I leave with you; my peace I give you. I do not give to you as the world gives. Do not let your hearts be troubled and do not be afraid.

Isaiah 26:3

Thou will keep him in perfect peace, whose mind is stayed on thee.

Luke 15: 10

In the same way, I tell you, there is rejoicing in the presence of the angels of God over one sinner who repents.

6. Tracking Achievements

After the divorce, in my early desperation days of confusion and no courage, I searched for vital truth in simple thoughts.

Instead of composing goals to achieve for the year, I started doing the opposite. Instead of *writing down goals* to achieve in one year in the future, I started *writing down achievements,* once a year, *after the year was over. Yes, achievements.*

You won't get a grade on this project until your life starts evolving into victory after victory. Is it really that easy to put things in writing? No. Is it really worth the effort? Yes… but *you have to try before you find out the truth. To verbalize helps you to actualize.*

I recommend that you record and remember Bluegrass Gospel Jam victories. Today is the most important day you have. What legacy of love can you leave behind?

Psalm 46: 1

God is our refuge and strength, an ever-present help in trouble.

Psalm 18: 49

Therefore I will praise you among the nations, O Lord; I will sing praises to your name.

Colossians 3: 16

Let the word of Christ dwell in you richly as you teach and admonish one another with all wisdom, and as you sing psalms, hymns and spiritual songs with gratitude in your hearts to God.

7. We Believe

We believe that music reaches souls when words alone cannot. No matter what your age, participation and encouragement revive the spirit within. We provide opportunities for spiritual growth. We encourage the development of unrecognized talents. We believe in the preservation of old gospel songs that have endured for many generations.

A Bluegrass Gospel Jam is an experience that can easily be shared with others. Gospel Jams provide the soothing balm of God's words set to music. The Bluegrass Gospel Jams were started to provide a place where families could have wholesome fun activities in a safe environment. My observation is that many modern families seldom gather together to just have good fun. Gospel Jams help folks slow down and enjoy and appreciate the time they have. Taking time *"to take time"* is what the Jams are all about.

In the Bluegrass Gospel Jam showground, many folks have family bands. Kids of all ages grow up playing and singing gospel music with their family. This is a tradition we want to promote and continue to foster. We are a *"Prevention of Problems Ministry."* We give the kids the chance to be included in the *"Outpost Ministry."* Participation develops into opportunities. Faith grows when it is practiced. Lives can change for the better. *Music, kids, people, musicians, God's spirit... that's a good combination, isn't it?*

Psalm 119: 11

I have hidden your word in my heart that I might not sin against you.

Psalm 51: 10

Create in me a pure heart, O God, and renew a steadfast spirit in me.

"You never know what you can do until you make up your mind and just do it." ...Unknown

"Inspiration comes when a new set of eyes views a normal situation through the eyes of God." ...Unknown

"Never reason from what you do not know. If you do, you will soon believe what is utterly against reason."... Ramsay

"Our prayers should be for blessings in general, for God knows what is good for us."... Socrates

Chapter 13 - "Tidbits Of Faith To Chew On"

1. Give Thanks With A Grateful Heart

Give thanks to God that you have been given the nudge and opportunity to consider starting a Bluegrass Gospel Jam. In the Bible, in the Old Testament, it was an obligation and essential part of tradition for parents to hand down values, virtues, and inheritance from generation to generation. You and I have an innate obligation to impart our spiritual heritage. It's like the Olympic torch. Now, it's your chance to carry the torch, pass it on, and keep the flame burning. With God in control, your partnership will always work out. A bluegrass gospel jam self-creates extraordinary friendships and camaraderie relationships. The successful jam leader sets the *"stage"* for victories. The triumphant jam leader sets the *"tone"* for triumphs.

2. Faith

How To Not Worry

I was fishing at a lake on a Saturday evening. I had been camping for two days. The summer day bathed me in sunshine. Towards evening, I decided to return to my campsite, about four miles away. The fishing outing had been peaceful for me. I was enjoying the solitude and quiet of the mountains. I stowed all my fishing gear into the back of my jeep. As I started up the jeep engine, I heard a loud *"clack-clack-clack"* coming from underneath the hood. As the jeep rolled forward, the noise increased even louder. I knew there was really something wrong this time. My thoughts raced. "*It sounds like the transmission is gone. Something is loose inside of the engine. My old jeep has had it. What am I going to do now?*"

All my thoughts were lonesome, worrisome, and scary. I was really in a pickle, now. I couldn't see any way out of my predicament. I was alone, totally alone. I worried into the encompassing night. On Thursday, five days later, I found out the problem. There was a plastic fan shroud that had split and was making contact with the engine fan. It was a minor problem that required a new part and twenty minutes to fix! *All my worries were unfounded and untrue!*

Worrying about the future is really very fruitless, isn't it? How can you worry about something that hasn't happened yet? I suggest that you seek out and know the facts first, before allowing worry to start. It's just a waste of time to worry about something that isn't a problem yet. A Bluegrass Gospel Jam can happen if you give the whole idea to God. Turn your worries over to God. He can handle them for you. Spend the time you save from not worrying - to figuring out how to get more out of today. Concentrate on the Bluegrass Gospel Jam victories. Guaranteed… the victories will far outnumber the worries.

Matthew 6: 25-27

Therefore I tell you, do not worry about your life, what you will eat or drink, or about your body, what you will wear. Is not life more important than clothes? Look at the birds of the air; they do not sow or reap or store away in barns, and yet your heavenly Father feeds them. Are you not much more valuable than they? Who of you by worrying can add a single hour to his life?

3. How to Become Rich

When I was recuperating from double bypass heart surgery, I had a lot of time to think, pray, and read. While in the hospital, I read a story that made me cry when I read it. The story was about a ten-year-old boy. His thirteen-year-old sister had a life-threatening illness and desperately needed a blood transfusion. Her illness required a blood transfusion of the same type from a family member. The boy was the only one in the family who had the correct blood type. When the doctor explained the situation to the boy, he thought about it for a while, and then said, *"OK. I'll do it."*

Later, as the little boy was laying on the hospital gurney beside his sister, as the transfusion was taking place, he asked the doctor, *"Doctor, now when do I die?"* The doctor immediately reassured him and replied, *"Oh no, son, you aren't going to die."* You see, the little boy thought he was giving *all* of his blood to his sister. Who is the rich person in this story? What does it mean to be rich?

There is no tomorrow! There is only today to be rich. The next generations can become poor in spirit and truth, just because of me, or just because of you. The next generations can also become rich, just because of me, or just because of you. *I live my life as if I were rich because I already am. "Rich" is how I feel and how I live my life.*

This affirmation is coming true more and more for me every year and day of my life. The Gospel Jam concepts evolved from these types of thoughts. I did not know at the time that I was laying the foundation for the formation of the Bluegrass Gospel Jam Network. The Bluegrass Gospel Jams are definitely a rich experience.

James 1: 2-4

Consider it pure joy, my brothers, whenever you face trials of many kinds, because you know that the testing of your faith develops perseverance. Perseverance must finish its work so that you may be mature and complete, not lacking anything.

Isaiah 26: 3

You will keep in perfect peace him whose mind is steadfast, because he trusts in you. Trust in the Lord forever, for the Lord, the Lord, is the rock eternal.

4. Thinking Power

In order to create an ongoing successful Bluegrass Gospel Jam, it is necessary to develop the concept of *"thinking time."* When you take time to think, creative inspiration can come in like a rushing wind. Part of your job as a leader is in preparing your own mind and spirit. Be open for revelation. *"Taking time to think"* creates peace. Can you effectively go forward sharing your vision thoughts of peace with the musicians surrounding you? Stop and think for a moment. When is your thinking time? Is your day or week so busy that you can't take time to stop and think?

Proverbs 3: 5-6

Trust in the Lord with all your heart and lean not on your own understanding; in all your ways acknowledge him, and he will make your paths straight.

How do you find peace through taking time to think your way through to starting a Bluegrass Gospel Jam? *Think about it!* The question presented is an answer in itself! You need not become confused. The answers to peace are already inside you. God put them there. You just have to take time to think about the answers, and then act.

Proverbs 16: 3-4

Commit to the Lord whatever you do, and your plans will succeed.

Psalm 29: 11

The Lord gives strength to his people; the Lord blesses his people with peace.

John 14: 7

Peace I leave with you; my peace I give you. I do not give to you as the world gives. Do not let your hearts be troubled and do not be afraid.

5. Adversities

Through faith, I have experienced being taken care of. It started with a choice. I chose to rely on God to help me through... I didn't choose to get angry when difficulties and adversities arose. I didn't choose to blame God for my circumstances. I didn't run away. I just prayed.

My good friend made this comment, *"You know, Ron, I used to pray and worry for you all the time. I don't worry about you any more. No matter what comes up, God takes care of you each time. This situation is only temporary. From what I have seen, God will take care of you."*

When you initiate a Gospel Jam, please recognize that you will have struggles along the way. There is an evil one out there ready to unleash his fury towards you. The evil one will try to undermine your efforts. The evil one doesn't want you to do anything worthwhile for God. He will tempt you at the weakest crevice of your character. He will try to make you give up and definitely cause you to become discouraged. Just be prepared for these *"road-block"* obstacles. They will surely happen. Realize that there is victory right around the corner. Prayers do work miracles. God wants you to be an overcomer. God wants you to be strong.

- Adversities should be viewed as *"opportunities to grow and learn."*
- Criticisms should be viewed as *"opportunities for course corrections."*
- Challenges should be viewed as *"opportunities to exercise faith."*
- Victories should be viewed as *"opportunities to share faith with others."*
- Gospel Jams should be viewed as *"opportunities to share God's word through music."*

John 14: 7

Peace I leave with you; my peace I give you. I do not give to you as the world gives. Do not let your hearts be troubled and do not be afraid.

Proverbs 14: 30

A heart at peace gives life to the body, but envy rots the bones.

Psalm 29: 11

The Lord gives strength to his people; the Lord blesses his people with peace.

6. Personal Affirmations

After having a double-bypass heart operation, I wrote down this affirmation in February of 1996. I review my many written affirmations often.

"I live as if I were rich (Rich is how I feel and how I live my life). Life is not about money. It's about time and how I spend money. Whether I

have little money or a lot of money, I spend it on the "free" things of life: Love, Beauty, Appreciation, Peace, Friendship, Caring, Family Time, Breathing Fresh Air, Walking, Listening to God and Nature and Music..."

I suggest you literally pray your way to victories. Remove the thoughts that you can do a more effective job all by yourself. It's much easier and more fun to let God lead. Most importantly, be sure to let everyone know that, *"This is God's Jam, not mine."* Courage in this manner pays huge dividends. It's a witness to others.

John 14: 7

Peace I leave with you; my peace I give you. I do not give to you as the world gives. Do not let your hearts be troubled and do not be afraid.

7. Who Do I Let In My Boat?

I made the positive choice to get more out of life and I am succeeding. I live a happy, healthy life because I now have peace and happiness in my heart and soul and mind. The only people I now let in my boat are caring friends.

Early on, one friend was creating misery for me and dragging my spirits down. *"I kicked him out of my boat."*

Sometimes this step is necessary to help you achieve peace. Make a choice. Choose to decide to stand up for what you believe. You can begin, now, to make positive choices for your life. Begin choosing on purpose the people and friends you want to be included in *"your boat."*

Think about the people you spend time with right now. Are there any positive outlook personalities? Do you spend time with negative or positive friends? Ask a high-quality friend sometime to observe and see if you are a positive or a negative personality. You can achieve anything when you surround yourself with good friends. Also be reminded that you can choose failure and frustration by choosing to associate with negative or non-encouraging friends.

Psalm 29: 11

The Lord gives strength to his people; the Lord blesses his people with peace.

Isaiah 26: 3

You will keep in perfect peace him whose mind is steadfast, because he trusts in you. Trust in the Lord forever, for the Lord, the Lord, is the rock eternal.

John 14: 27

Peace I leave with you; my peace I give you. I do not give to you as the world gives. Do not let your hearts be troubled and do not be afraid.

8. Generate Effective Emails

My most genuine effective *"people-contacting technique"* is email! When used in a proper manner, email saves time! Typically, a Bluegrass Gospel Jam leader is a one-person email communication coordinator. No one likes to receive *"junk"* email or *"spam"* email. The leader must develop simple blueprints that inform and communicate easily and quickly.

I use only *"Permission Granted"* email contact. I send email to only those who have signed up on the email roster. I also have an *"Opt Out"* feature provided in each message. Sometimes a person wants to discontinue receiving the emails. In that event, I immediately remove their name from the email roster. I only want people on the roster who enjoy receiving my emails.

My email roster continues to grow. How do you keep folks happy with your emails? As a refresher, here are some valuable tips that I have uncovered. I think I invented some of these terms!

Email Header Marketing

Place the entire core of your message in the subject line. That way, the message is communicated even if the recipient doesn't have the time or doesn't take the time to read right away, the whole email message.

Short And Sweet

We are in a speeding communication era. People who read emails are usually content with a quick glance. A large content article probably won't be read in its entirety. You need to become a succinct communicator using upbeat and encouraging words.

BCC

When sending out group-emails to your email roster, use the BCC *"Send To"* button. This method is called the Blind Carbon Copy (BCC). This procedure keeps the email addresses private and helps prevent others from capturing the email addresses of your group.

Respond ASAP

When receiving an email from a person from your group, try to respond as quickly as possible. In my way of thinking, instant communication is the primary purpose of email. Prompt response increases your credibility and concern for each individual behind the email.

Think thoroughly before sending the reply. When needed, before you reply, ask for clarification. Take time to say a short prayer before responding. Remember, you never really know what personal situation a person may be in.

Even if you have to think about it, at least respond with a phrase, *"Can you let me think about it before I give you a response?"* Acknowledging the person's effort to send you an email is much more important than ignoring the person… or giving a hasty *"non-thought-out"* reply. Procrastination is the primary source of aggravation for both the sender and receiver.

9. Email Core Value

Respond and communicate as quickly as possible

John 14: 27

Peace I leave with you; my peace I give you. I do not give to you as the world gives. Do not let your hearts be troubled and do not be afraid.

Psalm 37: 37

Consider the blameless, observe the upright; there is a future for the man of peace.

10. Encourage The Kids

From the outset, we encourage beginner musicians. There is rarely a place where beginner and average musicians can participate. When we all come together and play together, learning accelerates for everyone. Even when musicians don't know where the step of faith will lead, my job is to encourage people to try… and to step out. The gospel jams act as magnets, attracting both performer musicians and participating musicians of all ages.

The gospel jams offer a welcome respite for tired travelers, hurrying families, and people who don't have time for pure wholesome fun.

These are not my Jams... I have a partner relationship with God. I do the inviting and encouraging. God supplies the attendees and participants. Attracting youngsters is one of my personal goals. Would you like to participate in this endeavor?

James 1:5

If any of you lacks wisdom, let him ask of God...and it shall be given him.

Matthew 21:22

And all things, whatever ye shall ask in prayer, believing, ye shall receive.

11. Answers In Advance

Make an insert to include in your gospel jam flyer. Include *"frequently asked questions."* Here are some common questions. Summarize the most often asked questions and publish the answers in advance.

Samples:

- Do you charge for a Bluegrass Gospel Jam?

    All Jams are offered free of charge. Everyone is welcome.

- Do musicians have to try out before they are allowed to join in the Jams?

    We don't have auditions. We welcome all skill levels. All musicians who want to play are welcome to join in.

- Can people who sing, but don't play an instrument, join in, too?

Yes. We encourage singer participation.

- Are kids allowed to play and sing?

    Yes, we encourage all ages.

- When do you practice?

    We just show up and play together. That's the magic and mystery of the Jams.

- How are the Jams financed?

    Donation cans. Sometimes we sell various gospel jam apparel, CDs, and Start Up Songbooks. Folks are encouraged to give funds to support the movement. Sponsor Advertising is now being developed.

- Are the Jams acoustical only?

    Jams vary with every location. Some Jams are entirely acoustical. Some Jams have a mixture of both acoustical and amplified instruments. Jam leaders set the tone of each unique jam.

- How do you advertise the Jams?

    Email...Craig's List...Facebook...printed flyers...word of mouth personal invitation...

12. Carry Your Advertising Material With You At All Times

Just about every week, I receive questions and comments on the Gospel Jam logo displayed on the two rear windows of my car. This custom-designed logo decal has a banjo, music notes, a cowboy hat, and a cross in the background. I always carry extra flyers and invitation cards in my vehicle and weekly planner.

13. Official Logo Apparel

I suggest investing in a jacket with the Gospel Jam logo on both the front and back. I wear it all the time, to grandson baseball and basketball games, and tennis matches. I wear it when I go out to breakfast at a restaurant or shopping at the grocery store. It's a good idea to invest in both logo-imprinted long-sleeve and short-sleeved polo shirts. Blue denim shirts are very popular for Gospel Jam logo shirts. You can offer the imprinted shirts for a small markup to bring in funds for the jam. We also sell imprinted logo caps. Wherever a Jam leader or attendee goes, he or she can be a walking billboard, always inviting someone to a Bluegrass Gospel Jam. Folks do see you and will often ask, *"What is a Bluegrass Gospel Jam?"* It's your opportunity time to share and invite.

14. Stand Up Street Sandwich Sign

Invest in a folding metal sign to advertise on the street where your Jam will be held.

15. Business Cards

Create a business card with the name of your jam, the phone number, the email address, the logo, and your name as the leader and contact person. We created a heavy business card with a special finish that would allow a Jam member room to place his name. The business card increases referrals and recognition.

16. Display Table

Set up a display table so that you encourage purchases of logo apparel, songbooks, CDs, and other related Gospel Jam items. This table is the hub of information distribution. Have the email sign up sheet available.

17. Milk Can Donations

Purchase a couple of craft-store milk cans for the display table. Place a label on the cans requesting donations. A Jam cannot exist indefinitely without money coming in. Unless you have some kind of financial backer, you need to solicit funds to help with the expenses and growth of the gospel jams.

Hebrews 13: 1-2

Keep on loving each other as brothers. Do not forget to entertain strangers, for by so doing some people have entertained angels without knowing it.

Psalm 37: 37

…there is a future for the man of peace.

Psalm 66: 1-2

Shout with joy to God, all the earth! Sing the glory of his name; make his praise glorious.

18. Gathering Momentum

The development of new Bluegrass Gospel Jams is gathering momentum. There are clusters of bluegrass musicians just about anywhere you look. These are musicians who are looking for a place to play. Along with the right concept, all it takes is an organizer, some email, and a location. It's fun and rewarding to see simple ideas burst and grow into spectacular results.

19. A Movement

"We are a movement, not an organization." We want to help you and others get started with an effective ongoing Bluegrass Gospel Jam. You manage your own group of musicians and spectators. This guide you are reading provides you with hints on what works and doesn't work. In addition Jam leaders, from all over, share both *"victory stories"* and *"set-back stories."*

Proverbs 16: 9

In his heart a man plans his course, but the Lord determines his steps.

John 14: 27

Peace I leave with you; my peace I give you. I do not give to you as the world gives. Do not let your hearts be troubled and do not be afraid.

Ecclesiastes 8: 15

So I commend the enjoyment of life, because nothing is better for a man under the sun than to eat and drink and be glad. Then joy will accompany him in his work all the days of his life God has given him under the sun.

20. Instrument Workshops

I had lunch with a friend who told me her grandson wanted to learn to play a guitar. She asked if I knew of anyone. Here is a sample email request and response. The response came within one day.

Hello musicians,

We have a request for a 7-year old who wants to learn to play a guitar at the Jam on April 9.

He has use of a guitar, but he is an absolute beginner. If you would like to help him out, please let me know.

The instrument workshops are offered from 11:30 - 12:00 on Jam days.

Thanks,
Ron

Immediate Response:

Ron,

If you don't get anybody who is really qualified (I am NOT) then I can give it a try. At 7 his attention span will not be more than probably 15 to 30 min. I assume that would be the extent of the lesson?? Thoughts?

Craig

The grandmother was ecstatic when I informed her that her request had already been granted.

21. Choose Words Wisely

At first, I tried using the phrase, *"Beginning Instrument Lessons."* That phrase did not generate very many results. When I switched the concept to, *"Instrument Workshops,"* the instant response was amazing. We have plenty of rooms at our *"home-base"* Gospel Jam location. We are now making excellent use of those rooms for Instrument Workshops.

22. A Place To Learn

Musicians are always in a learning mode. Offering opportunities for musicians to improve and develop more skills generates even more genuine interest. Musicians tend to return when they are in a continual learning environment. That's what bluegrass gospel jams offer... a place to grow... in all ways.

2 Thessalonians 3: 16

Now may the Lord of peace himself give you peace at all times and in every way...

Psalm 14: 1

The fool says in his heart, "There is no God."

John 14: 27

Peace I leave with you; my peace I give you. I do not give to you as the world gives. Do not let your hearts be troubled and do not be afraid.

23. Instrumental Breaks

When you are leading the Jam, take time to instruct the musicians on *"how to take an instrumental break."* Most often, the instrumental break is taken right after the chorus. The person who chooses the song is the designated leader. That leader should guide (and stop singing) about five notes before the verse ends and announce loudly, for example, "*Fiddle*," or "*Banjo.*"

Singers and audience also have to be instructed to back off singing during the instrumental break and allow the instrumentalist to shine. I also will *"nod my head in advance"* to the musician when I want him or her to take the instrumental break. If the musician is watching, he will also nod that he or she has accepted the opportunity.

Proverbs 14: 30

A heart at peace gives life to the body, but envy rots the bones.

Luke 12: 29-31

And do not set your heart on what you will eat or drink; do not worry about it. For the pagan world runs after all such things, and your Father, knows that you need them. But seek first his kingdom, and all these things will be given to you as well.

Psalm 37:

Delight yourself in the Lord and he will give you the desires of your heart.

24. Inexperienced Guitar Player

God works in mysterious ways, mysterious at least to you and me. God took me, an inexperienced guitar player who couldn't tune a guitar, who couldn't keep a beat, who couldn't sing, and who definitely had no qualifications to lead a group of musicians, and let me become a leader of a growing phenomenon. I like my role as leader. I like the feeling that I am helping folks draw closer to God. I like welcoming in someone new.

I have discovered that the Bluegrass Gospel Jams are sometimes the only *"church"* some people will ever experience. I feel in my spirit that God is preparing other hearts to come and assist in this venture. I don't know whom, yet. I don't worry about it. *"God is in control."* This fact alone causes me to rejoice and smile.

1 John 2: 15-17

The world and its desires pass away, but the man who does the will of God lives forever.

Luke 12: 15

Watch out! Be on guard against all kinds of greed; a man's life does not consist in the abundance of his possessions.

Ecclesiastes 6: 12

Wisdom is a shelter as money is a shelter, but the advantage of knowledge is this: that wisdom preserves the life of its possessor.

25. Stress Removal

Formulating a Bluegrass Gospel Jam from scratch takes effort, diligence, fortitude, and courage. Stress can happen whenever you start any type of new venture. Taking a step without consulting God in prayer will definitely cause stress. However, when you actually turn your efforts over to God in prayer, in advance, you receive the immediate opportunity to travel the *"God-guided Gospel Jam Victory Trail."*

I continually have to focus on the outcomes and goals God has placed within my heart. I should say... my goals have God's blessings in my heart because I have turned over the outcome results to God.

Obstacles still surface now and then, but God and I continue to find even more positive paths on which to travel. Stress removal is like garbage removal. It has to be done at least once every week, or every day. Prayer is the first step to removing stress. The garbage truck comes through my alley very early in the morning, before most people are waking up. It makes an extremely rank roar of grinding and engine grumbling and banging around. I'm sure the garbage removal process can't afford to get behind schedule.

26. Peace Principles

Here are some practical peace principles to adhere to and believe in.

- The Gospel Jams flow much easier when you take a firm stand on what you actually believe.

- The Gospel Jams flow much easier when they are based upon peace outcome results.

- The Gospel Jams flow much easier when you pray ahead of time.

2 Thessalonians 3: 16

"Now may the Lord of peace himself give you peace at all times and in every way…"

Ephesians 4:26

In your anger do not sin. Do not let the sun go down while you are still angry, and do not give the devil a foothold.

27. Touching Lives With A Daily Bible Verse

I wanted to do something special for all the musicians and gospel jam attendees. Every morning, I began sending different single bible verse daily emails to everyone on the gospel jam roster. I chose all of my favorite verses that I had previously underlined in my bible. These chosen bible verses are fundamental in my own personal everyday life experiences. I call these verses, *"Bible Verse Blurbs Of Wisdom."*

Sending out these daily *"Bible Verse Blurbs Of Wisdom"* has been one of my most solid gospel jam building blocks. Everyone seems to appreciate my starting off his or her day with a bible verse. In fact, many folks have told me that they start off their morning devotions by first reading *"Ron's Bible Verse Blurbs Of Wisdom."*

Isaiah 55: 11

So is my word that goes out from my mouth: It will not return to me empty, but will accomplish what I desire and achieve the purpose for which I sent it.

I discovered that these selected bible verses have more impact than all of the information gospel jam emails I send. Almost every week, I receive responses like,

"Thanks, I really needed that today, or, "I was encouraged today by the bible verse."

Here are some examples of how God reaches people through me.

Thank you Ron for all the wonderful uplifting word. Had another chemo today. Came home and made soup for church tonight. The chemo will kick in tomorrow pm--I am ready with my shield and sword....

God bless you,

Verdyne

Harold is enjoying an afternoon of golf. He deserves an afternoon after being realtor/ mother/ wife/ cook .He sure has been my Right hand in more ways than one.

Hi Ron!

Thanks for the Cheerful heart proverb.

I started a small group of women in Loveland and we are probably going to call ourselves 'Cheerful Hearts." CH I almost went to Harmony Presbyterian Sunday morning.

Blessings,

Carrie G.

I love your Blurbs, Ron. They seem to be right on time in their message.

Peace!
Saja

Hello Ron and good to hear from you. Apologize not getting back to you soon.

Stay busy most the time at work and home. A lot of things going on. Hope one day to see you and that thanks for all the INFO and websites you send. Looks like the our Lord is taking care of your needs.

Best Regards, Kirk

Thank you Ron... needed this today!! The strength is amazing- God is sooo good and is using you to get "it" out.

Thanks again

" Because He Lives " :) Zella

Hi Ron, We are doing better this week. I had an operation the 26 of Aug. and am going in for a post op. appointment today. Starting to feel much better now. I read your Bible Verse every day and want to say thanks for posting them. Carol

Good Morning, Ron

And for you.... "Continuous effort - not strength or intelligence - is the key to unlocking our potential." Winston Churchill

28. How's Your Week Going?

Periodically, I sit down at my computer and review the gospel jam email roster. I say a prayer over the list. I send out this question, *"How's Your Week Going?"* I only send this special email if I definitely feel God is directing me to do so. The responses flood back in. I know the recipients appreciate my taking the time to communicate with them. The responses are usually short, but I get a glimpse of what's happening in their life. This step helps bond us together with minimum effort on my part. I always send a response immediately, thanking them for the update. I offer encouragement at every opportunity.

I often receive requests for prayer for all kinds of illness, cancer, loved ones, and hard family situations. I'm not a pastor. I reply right away by typing out a reply prayer for that person indicating that I will be praying for them. Again, it is important to respond as quickly as possible. In the future I will be seeking out persons who thrive upon helping out by praying for people in need of prayer.

Take the time to personally care for your flock of musicians and audience. The question, *"How is your week going?"* shows that you care.

Colossians 3: 15

Let the peace of Christ rule in your hearts, since as members of one body you were called to peace. And be thankful.

29. All Things Are Possible

I believe God is using me to lead and to show others that *all things are possible when you take a step forward for God*. I feel God's presence in the Jams. This feeling makes me smile inside and out. This feeling helps me meet and greet new people with a genuine welcoming spirit. It's fun and rewarding being an ambassador for God.

You don't have to be a good performer to enjoy music. How do you think professional performers achieved what they now do? Practice. But I ask you, practice for what? Why not throw off that, *"I've got to be perfect before I try"* routine? Amidst the hustle-bustle, how about experiencing some quality and valuable fun now, today, this week, this month?

A Bluegrass Gospel Jam is truly, *"An Outpost Ministry with No Walls."* All you have to do is pray, start, and begin inviting folks to come. Please remember, *"You do the inviting. God supplies the attendees."*

Can you agree with me on this concept? If so, I encourage you to form a new Bluegrass Gospel Jam. Musicians are out there, just waiting for you to give them an opportunity. Become an encourager. Share your victories. Seek, find, and depend upon God's guidance.

Plant the mustard seeds of faith, and watch them grow! It happened for me. It can happen for you, too. Remember… we have no walls! Come and join me in spreading the gospel all over the USA and beyond.

Psalm 46: 1

God is our refuge and strength, an ever-present help in trouble.

1 Peter 5:7

Cast all your anxieties on him because he cares for you.

James 5: 13

Is any one of you in trouble? He should pray. Is anyone happy? Let him sing songs of praise.

30. Relying Upon The Bible For Daily Wisdom

Colossians 3: 15

Let the peace of Christ rule in your hearts, since as members of one body you were called to peace. And be thankful. Let the word of Christ dwell in you richly as you teach and admonish one another with all wisdom, and as you sing psalms, hymns, and spiritual songs with gratitude in your hearts to God. And whatever you do, whether in word or deed, do it all in the name of the Lord Jesus, giving thanks to God the Father through him.

31. More "Bible Verse Blurbs Of Wisdom"

Psalm 51: 10

Create in me a pure heart, O God, and renew a steadfast spirit in me.

Philippians 4: 6

Do not be anxious about anything, but in everything, by prayer and petition, with thanksgiving, present your requests to God. And the peace of God, which transcends all understanding, will guard your hearts and minds in Christ Jesus.

1 Thessalonians 5: 18

Be joyful always; pray continually; give thanks in all circumstances, for this is God's will in Christ Jesus.

1 John 5: 14

This is the confidence we have in approaching God: that if we ask anything according to his will, he hears us. And, if we know that he hears us- whatever we ask- we know we have what we asked of him.

Philippians 4: 4-7

Rejoice in the Lord always. I will say it again: Rejoice! Let your gentleness be evident to all. The Lord is near. Do not be anxious about anything, but in everything, by prayer and petition, with thanksgiving, present your requests to God. And the peace of God, which transcends all understanding, will guard your hearts and your minds in Christ Jesus. Finally, brothers, whatever is true, whatever is noble, whatever is right, whatever is pure, whatever is lovely, whatever is admirable – if anything is excellent or praiseworthy – think about such things.

Ecclesiastes 4: 6

Better one handful with tranquility than two handfuls of toil and chasing after the wind.

2 Thessalonians 3: 16

Now may the Lord of peace himself give you peace at all times and in every way…

John 14: 27

Peace I leave with you; my peace I give you. I do not give to you as the world gives. Do not let your hearts be troubled and do not be afraid.

Proverbs 14: 30

A heart at peace gives life to the body, but envy rots the bones.

Proverbs 14: 15

A simple man believes anything, but a prudent man gives thought to his steps.

Chapter 14 - My Bluegrass Gospel Jam Journey

How I Got Started

This is a firsthand demonstration of what can happen when someone begins attending a Bluegrass Gospel Jam. If you, as a prospective leader, choose to grab hold of God's hand, the opportunity to reach others for God... will be in your hands.

"Ron, what do you think about this real estate deal?" asked Ray.

I answered, *"Ray, I need to tell you something. I'm going through a divorce. I'm really not in a good frame of mind, nor am I in a neutral position, to be able to advise you. I really need the commission money. I can tell you that this deal makes sense on strictly a real estate level, but I can't help you decide. This is one decision that you will have to make on your own."*

"OK!" Ray replied.

The real estate market at that time was bleak. For almost ten years, the whole market had been in a dreary struggle for survival. During this frazzled time, Ray was one of my best real estate clients. He was making offers on real estate when no one else would venture out. He was also my most exasperating client. His purchases took more energy, long discussions, more late-night cups of coffee, and more time than the rest of all my sales combined. A friend of mine, another real estate salesman, told me that he would have *"fired"* Ray a long time ago, if he had to put up with all the grief Ray caused for me. My friend would not have been able to work with Ray.

The next day, Ray called me and said, *"OK, go ahead and draw up the offer."*

It was a complicated transaction, involving owner financing and *"cross-collateral"* with another piece of real estate. The transaction took about three months to close. During this time, I had terrible, splitting, painful headaches. I was going through the beginnings of an unexpected divorce. I had moved to an apartment. Real estate sales were down. I was working harder and longer with fewer results. The financial scramble was stressful and distressing. I thought I could work my way out of the drowning real estate market. I was wrong. The headaches and strain caused me to know that I needed to do something do start dealing with the pain.

I called up Harold, my former real estate boss and mentor. Harold lived in Mesa, Arizona at the time. *"Hi, Harold, this is Ron. I have a question for you. Where's the best real estate market in the country?"*

"Call Mark." Mark was Harold's son. *"Mark lives in Las Vegas and is selling new homes for a builder out there. Las Vegas is the best real estate market in the country."*

I called Mark and he confirmed what Harold had told me. Mark also said that it probably would be easy to get on with a builder out there. I made up my mind to move to Las Vegas, obtain my Nevada Broker's license, and to sell new houses for builders. This abrupt decision was not typical of my personality. I never made major decisions like this without lots of thought and deliberation. I was not a spur-of-the moment decision maker. I was desperate. I was in a daze, running around in a vicious circle, with nowhere to go. The sale with Ray closed and I received one of my larger commission checks. It was the end of September. I negotiated my way out of my apartment lease. I sold or gave away as many big things as I could. I packed all my remaining belongings into my small gas-mileage-efficient Honda car.

My good friend, Luke, had just moved his real estate office to his home. I asked if he needed a file cabinet. Luke made the offer to me, *"Instead of paying you for the file cabinet, how about doing a trade? You have always said you wanted a guitar. How about trading the file cabinet for the guitar?"* I agreed. I tucked in the guitar on top of the rest of my stuff in my Honda. I headed west to Las Vegas. On the way out of town, I stopped at a music store. I purchased 5 cassette tapes. It was the first time I had ever purchased something for myself. The rest of the time, I had worked to provide for my family. On the way to Las Vegas, I turned off the radio. I played the tapes over and over. The radio in my vehicle has never been turned on again.

I listen to music now, all of the time. Music makes me peaceful now. I don't keep up on the news much. News just doesn't seem to matter any more. I buy lots of music now. I listen a lot. I rented an apartment in Las Vegas and proceeded to go to real estate school to obtain my Broker's license. While I was going to school, I traversed Las Vegas daily, passing out my card to every builder and open house salesman I could find. While I drove, I listened to my music.

2 Thessalonians 3: 16

Now may the Lord of peace himself give you peace at all times and in every way…

Las Vegas was bustling with activity. In order to get signed up for utilities, the power company had to have a policeman directing traffic to guide cars in and out. Inside, everyone in line was served coffee and donuts to make all the new customers comfortable. Homebuilders were everywhere. Subdivisions were popping up like popcorn. Every street was lined with signs, directing everyone to the new show homes.

It was a hard time for me in Las Vegas. It was a lonely time. I tried to rent furniture but the rental store turned me down because I didn't have a job. I purchased an air mattress and pump so I would have a bed. I agonized for a week before purchasing a small TV. I was afraid to spend any money. I still had monthly bills coming in, and now, no income. I agonized equally over buying a chair to sit in. I finally purchased a folding chair with a padded seat for about $15.00. To eat meals, I sat on the floor with a pillow at my back. I had a nice apartment with lots of room- and no furniture. I set up my computer and office in the bedroom on top of the empty apple boxes I had used to pack all my things. I started faxing my résumés to the builders. I ate lunch at Taco Bell every day because I could buy 2 burritos and water for $1.47.

Walking was my only activity. I walked around the subdivisions on big wide winding sidewalks. All the new houses had stucco fences circling around them. The subdivision streets were wide and curved. In Las Vegas, the cars never really stopped at the stop signs. Most of the time the cars slowed down and rolled on through, *"a rolling stop."* There were man-made lakes all around, but very seldom were there any people out or by the lakes. In fact the high stucco fences, the beautiful homes, and the *"rolling stops,"* appeared to offer only a temporary respite from working all day, and night. It was as if I were walking among individual castles with the moats being out in the center.

To help fill in time, instead of driving to the grocery store, I walked. I found a grocery store that had a delicatessen where I could buy a cheap breakfast. I invested in an insulated coffee mug that was refillable at a cheap price. I did all my studying for real estate at the delicatessen. There were not a lot of people up early in the morning, so I had lots of peace and quiet. At that time I started a morning ritual that I still follow to this day. I began every morning, by reading the Bible. Back then, I read 5 chapters of the Bible per day. Also, I read 5 daily devotions from Billy Graham, 2 pages of

"Promises from the Bible", and one chapter of Norman Vincent Peale's, *"The Power of Positive Thinking."*

I prayed every morning. I didn't know what was ahead of me, but I figured that, if I started out with God every morning, that at least I had started out the day right. I have since doubled my reading. It takes about an hour every morning. I drove the whole city of Las Vegas, prospecting for a job. My music was my only companion. I found that the job-finding process was not as easy as I had envisioned. I discovered that the real estate builders in Las Vegas had big corporate shells protecting them. It was taking too much time. I was running out of time…and money.

I talked to my friend, Luke, back home. In fact, Luke was always calling me long distance. He knew I couldn't afford to call him. I explained my dilemma of not being able to penetrate the *"corporate core"* situation and asked for his assistance. Luke had always been good at marketing. He came up with a brilliant, I thought, low cost way for me to get noticed. Luke told me to go to a music store and buy some guitar picks. He said to put one pick in each envelope with a letter from me stating, *"When it's time to choose your next real estate salesman, I hope you will pick me!"*

The next day, I went down to Wal-Mart and had my picture taken. I wore my best suit and tie. I put the guitar I had traded for, around my neck, holding a guitar pick in my hand. I chose the cheapest picture package with the most photos. A few days later, I began sending out my résumés with the picture of me in my suit, with my guitar. Some builders got large photos; some got small pictures.

During this time I also went to church. I found a small church, not too far away, right in the center of a bunch of new subdivisions. I attended every service, every social function, men's group, or dinner. I needed help fitting in, quickly. One time, I was feeling extremely low in spirit. I started driving around the parking lot, on Wednesday evening, at dusk, waiting for that church to open. It seemed an eternity, waiting for that church to open. I don't know what would have happened if people hadn't started showing up. I got to ask for prayer that night in a small group, and I made it through the night.

Christmas was a downer for me. My two daughters and grandkids sent me a small tree and presents, but I was very much *"all-alone."* It's a vacant hollow feeling to be alone and lonesome. No matter how I tried to occupy my time, I just missed *"normalcy."* I sat there, pondering my plight, when the phone rang. It was Mark. He invited me to his house to have Christmas dinner with his family! I accepted. He also told me that his dad and mom, Harold and Verdyne, were flying out from Arizona. I really appreciated being with friends on Christmas. It was as if they knew I needed help in my time of despair and loneliness.

On the day after Christmas, I grabbed a couple of oranges and stuck them in my coat pocket. I started out on my daily walk. I walked twice a day now, to fill in the time. I had nothing to do. All my prospective job letters had been sent out and I was getting no immediate response. It was the wrong time of the year to be looking for a job. It was the holidays, between Christmas and New years. Everybody in the business world goes on vacation during the holidays. It was cold and the wind was blowing. The sun was out and offered a small portion of radiant warmth. I sat on a chilly cement bench, beside one of the lakes, peeling an orange. I was praying. It was quiet. I don't even know what my prayer was specifically about. Does prayer always have to be about something specific? Is there a possibility that God knows a lot more about what to do, than you do? Is there a possibility that God comes to your aid when you need the help the most? I sat there on the concrete bench for a long time. Finally, I began getting the feeling, *"You have to go back."* The thought persisted. After a few days, I decided to go back. I called Luke and told him what my plans were.

"What do you plan doing when you get back?" he asked.

"I don't know. All I know is that I'm coming back."

I informed the apartment management company that my job situation in Las Vegas had not worked out. I tried to negotiate out of my apartment lease. It was not easy. I had to pay a lot more rent after I left. I loaded up the Honda again with all the re-packed apple boxes and headed back to Colorado. My music accompanied me all the way back. The guitar rode on top of the apple boxes. When I arrived back to Colorado, on a Sunday evening, I had coffee with Ray. I had $780 in my pocket. I had bills coming due in 3 days amounting to over $3600. I had nowhere to live.

"Where are you going to stay, Ron?" asked Ray.

"I don't know. I was hoping I could stay in the basement of your house for a night. Then I could try to find something on Monday."

"Do you have any money?"

I told him my situation. I ended up staying in Ray's basement for quite a while. There was no shower. I went daily to the public swimming pool to take a shower. At first, there was no stove or refrigerator. I found out that milk stays cold when you store it in the snow.

Instead of agonizing over real estate sales, I decided to try doing mortgage loans for a living. At that time, all my real estate clients weren't buying or selling. They were all refinancing their house loans. The mortgage loan business caused a lot more stress for me. In addition, the person I worked for was not an honorable person and he backed out of paying me over $6,000 in commissions that I had earned.

All in all, my life was not going anywhere. Have you had times when you didn't know which way to turn? Have you ever felt that you couldn't even think about setting goals again? Have you ever felt so depressed that you couldn't even show up in small claims court to fight for what was rightly yours?

My music still accompanied me when I was driving around. Music was just about my only refuge. The guitar sat at home in the corner, by itself, in my makeshift apartment. I made trips to the mountains, often, with music playing. I tried to find some peace and sense to life.

Psalm 37: 37

Consider the blameless, observe the upright; there is a future for the man of peace.

As I began trying to learn to live alone, (just to exist really), I found a group of musicians that played gospel music every other Thursday evening. The gathering was called a *"Bluegrass Gospel Jam."* I had never been to a *"jam"* before. I went several times and just listened. They were playing songs I had learned in church, but doing it in a fast bluegrass style. Musicians and spectators, alike, were all having a good time. A photocopied, stapled-together songbook had been passed out. The audience would choose and request their favorite song. Each song had all the words to all the verses. The audience joined in song as the musicians played and sang. Entire families came. It was a family event.

I finally mustered up enough courage to take my guitar to the evening sessions. I couldn't tune the guitar, because I couldn't discern the variation in one note over another. I could only tell if the guitar was in tune. I couldn't even begin to try to make it sound right. I started asking the other musicians to tune my guitar for me. I would say, *"Boy, I just can't seem to get this guitar tuned!"* I didn't know how! The best thing about a *"jam"* is that anyone is allowed to play along. Whether a beginner or an old timer, no one cares. Music still comes out and everyone gets to practice while they learn.

I knew about 3 finger positions for the chord of *"G."* Most of those early songs were done in *"G."* I couldn't finger fast. I couldn't tell when the finger positions were supposed to change. I couldn't strum to the music. I had *"zero"* music ability. Singing was completely out of my capability. I enjoyed just being with the group. I started sitting across from other guitar players and watched as they moved their fingers to the new chord positions. I still do that today when I play.

Psalm 29: 11

The Lord gives strength to his people; the Lord blesses his people with peace.

Most of all, I started paying attention to the words to all those good old church songs. Music was connecting to my soul and I was beginning to participate. In the past I never really listened to the words of songs. I retained some of the melodies in my head, I guess, and words and melodies evidently settled somewhere in my subconscious. Words never meant much, until now. Music made the words come alive. Have you ever read the words of the Bible? Then, like lightning, a light comes on in your mind, and you say, *"Wow, I didn't see that meaning before!"* Suddenly the words of the Bible start taking residence in your mind. The lamp of understanding starts shining through to your subconscious. Is it possible that this is the way God actually *"speaks"* to you and me?

The gospel jam gathering made me feel connected. The music was soothing and the words started reassuring me. Without knowing, I had just begun the process of healing. It was frustrating that I couldn't make chords, or strum, or catch on to the rhythm, but I felt something that drew me in to music.

Every other week, the highlight of that week was going to that Thursday night jam. On the way home, I would turn on my tape player and play classical music all the way home. I used to laugh at myself, at the contradiction of playing bluegrass country music in one moment, and playing classical music all the way home. The style of the music didn't matter. Music is music and who can doubt the impact on each and every person? What would your world be like, if there were no more music? Who do you think invented music? If music can stir our emotions, is it entirely possible for God to *"speak"* to you through music?

Playing a guitar was a far cry from playing a trombone in the marching band in high school. I really struggled to keep up with the bluegrass musicians. These guys were good! Everyone was always having a good time. I found out that everyone was willing to help me. Most of all, I received continual encouragement. I will never forget the night at the jam when I developed my *"first personal strum."* Earlier, many people had shown me how to strum, but none of those styles worked for me. I just couldn't get it. I even went to a community college night class to learn how to strum. Nothing worked until that one night. The mastery I felt surpassed all my imagination. I could actually strum! I don't know where my strum came from; it just sort of *"happened."* It was something I could do to play along with the others. I still couldn't get the chord changes. That was still way above my abilities.

I continued learning at the Thursday night jams. I started attending the same church my wife and I and our family had attended before the divorce. Now, I was an *"outsider"* coming into church. I was now a divorced, single man. I didn't fit in. I decided that I needed to do something to stay active in church. I wanted to do something special to attract new people to church. Encouraging new people to go to church has always been my passion. I am an encourager. Have you identified something you would like to do for God? What is your passion? Does a person have to have a particular skill fully developed before starting to do work for God?

Over coffee at a restaurant, I decided to do a gospel jam at church. I chose Sunday nights, for two reasons. When I attended church for the first time, it was on a Sunday night. I enjoyed the lively music when I first walked in. In that particular church, every person who wanted to play was allowed to perform in the band. There were guitars, trumpets, flutes, fiddles, base guitars, and a collage of all kinds of other instruments. The second reason for choosing Sunday nights was to increase the attendance on Sunday nights at my church. I received permission to make an announcement about what I was planning to accomplish.

"My goal," I announced, *"is to have more people here at church on Sunday evening, than the number who attend on Sunday morning! It will probably never happen, once we get new people coming on Sunday nights. I figure that the church will automatically start growing very quickly."*

This was my self-imposed challenge. And I could just barely play my guitar. I created a poster flyer with tear-off slips. I advertised:

Bluegrass Gospel Jam Now Forming

- Beginners and Experienced
- Perform at Various Events
- Practice at 5:00 Perform at 6:OO Sunday Nights

I put up the flyer on a bulletin board at a nearby grocery store. I also put up a flyer on a Christian bookstore's bulletin board. Almost immediately, I started receiving phone calls from interested musicians and singers. Beginners and experienced performers started coming. I encouraged the people in my church, especially kids and young adults, to come up front and help perform. Soon on Sunday nights, there were more performers up on the stage than there were attendees sitting in the pews. I figured the more people I could get, the more I would be able to blend in with my amateur guitar playing!

Proverbs 14: 30

A heart at peace gives life to the body, but envy rots the bones.

Someone from another church called and said they were putting a *"Bluegrass Mass"* together for one particular Sunday. They wanted me to be in their bluegrass group. *"Wow, I can barely play, and now I'm in two groups."* When you take a leap of faith, do you believe that the Lord will lay out a path for you? I was becoming excited now! I was now fulfilling a passion that I had only dreamed about. I was becoming successful at inviting new people to church! The *"Bluegrass Mass"* group grew in size to about 15 people. We were good! I learned some beautiful new songs. I came up with a new plan. I invited the whole group over to my church to perform on Sunday evening on the same Sunday they were playing for their own Sunday morning *"Bluegrass Mass."*

Their pastor surprised me that Sunday morning when he invited his whole huge congregation, and their friends, to hear more bluegrass gospel music that evening. I had talked my church into having a chili supper after the service to make it a very special Sunday evening. After that pastor's announcement, I had to scramble around and tell everyone to make more chili. *"We are going to have a lot of people!"*

Sunday evening came. We had more people in the church than ever before. The church was packed! We combined both bluegrass groups, and we each did our songs. The church was filled with an evening of music and fun. We celebrated after the event with the chili supper. A lot of people made new friends. My dream had come to fruition. I achieved the goal of surpassing the number of people who attended on Sunday morning. I was elated!

The thrill didn't last long! Some of the people at my church didn't like what happened. For some reason, my bringing in people from another church caused difficulty for them. My motives were good, but the surprise of the event overtook their emotions. *"Too many people up on the stage..."* was one of the objections. They balked at the entire concept. Then, I found out from the pastor that *"they were going to fire the pastor if I continued with this type of activity."*

Galatians 5: 22

But the fruit of the Sprit is love, joy, peace, patience, kindness, goodness, faithfulness, gentleness, and self-control.

I was devastated. In my mind, so many good things had happened! The pastor, and his wife were good people. They were good friends to me. I even had the pastor playing his guitar up front on Sunday evenings. He and his wife were singing in the bluegrass gospel group. I told the pastor and his wife, *"I love doing this music thing, but I'm not going to continue if your job is in jeopardy!"* I quit. The church still fired the pastor. Later on, over coffee with the pastor, I asked him what happened.

"Ron, I knew I was in trouble about two weeks after I got here to take over the church. After that first board meeting, I knew something was wrong, but I didn't know what to do."

"How is it working out at your new church? What is the difference?" I asked.

"I don't know, Ron. I'm still the same person. They just like me."

It took a long time for me to get over this incident. I had to learn over time how to forgive.

Matthew 5:9

Blessed are the peacemakers, for they will be called the sons of God.

What do you do when you run into adversity like this? *I quit going to church for about seven months.* I figured I could still read my Bible and pray, without going to church. During this period, I did another curious thing. I went down to the Christian bookstore where I had placed the *"Gospel Jam"* flyer. I took out a yellow pad. I wrote:

Intermediate Guitar Player (I lied a little)

- Wants to play bluegrass gospel music.

- Sunday nights would be ideal. Call Ron.

I pinned the yellow piece of paper to the bulletin board. About two months later, I received a call from Mike, a young music pastor. His wife had seen my yellow pad note. Mike and his wife were planting a new church. Mike and I met for coffee, and our personalities connected right away. I decided to help Mike and his wife bring in new people to his church. We started *"Picnics in the Park."* We chose a time, picked a spot under a picnic gazebo alongside a walking and riding trail. We invited other musicians. We had free fried chicken. We had a successful concert with guest musicians and friends. Mike and his wife were former professional musicians. They let me play with them. Our music styles were entirely different, but that didn't matter. I became the booking agent and we started playing music everywhere someone would invite us. Then, I formed *"Grand Kids Country Church."* Every year I invited both young and old to perform. I combined bluegrass music with whatever talent I could uncover. I encouraged everyone to come and participate. *"I have found that people will come and perform, if they are asked, and if encouraged to come."*

The yellow pad pinned to the Christian bookstore's bulletin board was my effort to serve God. God answered my prayer and brought into my life a music pastor and friend. How would I have ever known that I was going to be helping out Mike later on down the road? Do you know in advance what is ahead of you when you start doing God's will?

Ephesians 5: 19-20

Speak to one another with psalms, hymns and spiritual songs. Sing and make music in your heart to the Lord, always giving thanks to God the Father for everything in the name of Jesus Christ.

Music has become a part of my life. I play at bluegrass and country jams every Sunday afternoon now. I'm still learning. My goal is to make gospel music an exciting part of the rest of my life. It's so fun, rewarding, and peaceful to me. I believe the Lord has more plans for me. I don't know for sure just what, but I'm open. The Lord has shown me the way, all through the troubles of life, and I have never really lacked for anything. I don't have to worry. I have peace. I'm finding even more peace through music. I'm getting younger. I'm getting healthier. It's sure nice having a friend like Jesus. Life is so much easier when you let God lead. Do you still try to do everything on your own or do you let God lead? Can you visualize training your thoughts away from thoughts of failure and towards thoughts of possibilities? I'm 61 years old and I've even started singing…out loud… and into a microphone! What a miracle!

Living a Christ-centered life, a believing life, and a life of faith are normal events. They are not some type of supernatural phenomena. If you act upon true faith principles, your life will become fruitful for God. Without true faith and belief in God, life really does become meaningless, hollow, with no substance, and without peace. The truth is that belief, faith, and peace come from the hand of God. Yes, man has been created with a choice, but man has to discern what truth is. Other than really believing in God, real truth can't exist without God. The story of God is all laid out in the Bible, for each of us to read and believe. Sooner or later, we do have to read. We all need, sooner or later, to believe. We all need, sooner or later, help. We all want, sooner or later, the valuable things in life.

For some reason, man's total existence on earth is spent on discovering the truth to life. When a man finds truth, he sometimes doesn't think it is possible to find such an easy answer. Faith, belief, salvation, Jesus, all point to you and me living a more rewarding, happy, and faith-filled life. Sometimes we keep on working at *"finding"* life instead of rejoicing with *"found"* life. Through my real-life experiences, I have made some momentous decisions. In a self-improvement book, I read that you have to *"learn to like your job."* This is good advice, but I have an even more powerful principle. I simply decided that, if I have to work or do something, *"I'm going to do something I enjoy doing!"* I started a quest to ask myself what I truly enjoyed doing. That's how music became a part of my life. I didn't have the skills, but I had the desires to enjoy. I decided that I enjoyed teaching, so I became a part time teacher in a real estate licensing school. I decided I liked fishing and camping, so I have become known as *"Ron, the fisherman."* I enjoy writing, so I write these books on peace. I enjoy my grandkids, so I have become *"the greatest Papa around."*

I enjoy sharing my faith with people. I enjoy helping people start to believe, and to come to church for the first time. I enjoy being an encourager. I enjoy being on God's team. As I think about it, I really supremely enjoy being *"who I am."* It's taken a long gradual time to find out *"who I am."* It all started with searching out what made sense and discovering what was valuable in life. Life is a choice, so why not make a decision to choose what makes you happy? Combine your inner desires with guidance from God and you will find yourself on the same team with me, *"God's team."*

"You don't have to get good before you join the team; you just have to play your heart out."

It's all in the Bible. You and I simply can change and begin accepting the *"real truth."* It's really the simplest thing that there is to do. Practicing an overcoming and victorious type life sometimes takes a while, but it is certainly worth the resulting victories.

I didn't have to know all about guitar playing before I liked music.

I didn't have to know all about Grandpas before I became *"the greatest Papa, ever."*

I didn't have to become an expert on fishing before I enjoyed fishing.

I didn't have to become a famous author before I just sat down and started writing these books for you to read.

Life is all in the *"doing"* and the *"practicing."* Why not seek out what you truly enjoy? Become passionate about something, pray to God, practice joy, and you are already on God's team. Leave the decisions to God. He will give you the sign to *"bunt"* or *"hit away."*

Psalm 150: 1-6

Praise the Lord. Praise God in the sanctuary; praise him in his mighty heavens. Praise him for his acts of power; praise him for his surpassing greatness. Praise him with the sounding of the trumpet, Praise him with the harp and lyre, Praise him with tambourine and dancing, Praise him with the strings and the flute, Praise him with the clash of cymbals, Praise him with resounding cymbals. Let everything that has breath praise the Lord. Praise the Lord.

Starting Over

After the 7-month period of not going to a church anywhere, Mike continued to invite me to the church he attended. Because I was still hurting over what happened at my home church, I really hesitated to accept the invitation. Mike's church promoted the formation of small groups. Mike continued to invite me to the Sunday evening small group. Finally, when Mike kept on encouraging me with, *"Ron, they have food!"* I summoned the courage to join in. Mike was the music pastor for his church.

Eventually, I received permission to do gospel jams every other Saturday night in the fireplace fellowship room. On that first jam night, three musicians came. No one from the church came. Mike and his wife didn't show up. The youth pastor and his family lived in the back of the church. They didn't even poke their head into the fellowship room. The chairs I set up were empty.

During the next two weeks, I emailed the few musicians I had on the roster from the previous regular bluegrass jams I had attended. The response was almost non-existent. On the night of the *second* jam, it was 6:30, starting time. No one was there. I had to make a decision. *"What do I do now, Lord?"* Standing at the microphone, I began singing my favorite songs, trying to find the appropriate chords on my guitar. I couldn't sing but I sang anyway. I couldn't play my guitar. I closed my eyes. At 6:45, no one was there. At 6:55, Jeremy, one of the musicians from the previous jam came in with his guitar.

"Light turnout huh, Ron?"

About the time Jeremy got out his guitar, we heard car doors slamming out in the parking lot. Musicians and musician families and friends started flowing in. We ended up with about thirty people. My pallid discouragement turned to joy.

Isaiah 26: 3

You will keep in perfect peace him whose mind is steadfast, because he trusts in you. Trust in the Lord forever, for the Lord, the Lord, is the rock eternal.

2 Thessalonians 3: 16

Now may the Lord of peace himself give you peace at all times and in every way...

My First Fundamental Commitment

My resolve, from that point on, was that I would sing and play anyway, *"even if there were empty chairs, or if no musicians showed up."* I dedicated myself to playing the good old gospel songs to God, regardless of who or how many showed up. Starting out can be very lonely. Really, you aren't alone. You are doing work for God. His presence is there. By faith, you just have to believe. God honors your diligence. So don't be discouraged easily. Be encouraged. You are preparing for victories. God wants you to mature.

Rescued From Despair

The very first bluegrass gospel jams I attended actually rescued me out of momentous misery and personal despair. Even though I felt *"gloomy about myself,"* the words of the songs kept reassuring me that God was present. As a leader, you will get plenty of experience in observing how people's lives change just because of the presence of a gospel jam. *In the midst of my desperation*, the bluegrass gospel music brought me comfort, peace, encouragement, and a sense of belonging. Since that time, my goal has been to share that same experience with others.

I Wasn't As Lost As Before

Do you have some musical experience? There was no musical ability on my part. My emotions were crawling along the bottom of the creek. Working with artistic musicians didn't offer much supporting encouragement. I had no leadership training to assist and guide me. I felt totally inadequate. Coordinating and trying to lead musicians was not my expertise. I didn't know *"keys"* or *"chords."* As I stated above, all I could understand, was that gospel music was undergirding my spirit, drawing me closer and closer to God. God's spirit started reaching my heart through the words and melodies. *I felt like I wasn't as lost as before.* Even though fear was rampant, I soon became a man full of passion for music. I wasn't born a leader or a musician. I just learned as I went along.

Greater Than Ever Faith

Each individual gospel jam provides an excellent opportunity for developing *"greater-than-ever faith."* From my perspective, with faith as the foundation, gospel jams built entirely upon Bible scriptures... will endure. Each time I try to place my own ideas into action, I often find myself haltingly trying to figure out the next step with the jams. I continually have to remind myself to pray for the people who will be coming. I rely on prayer to supersede my efforts as the leader.

Reviving Passion

My stated passion is to guide non-believers and fringe believers to get to know God in a practical easy-to-understand way. Bluegrass gospel jams help fuel that passion. My passion is to invite. It's easier for me, and for most folks, to invite new people to a gospel jam, rather than to invite them to a church. Most church attendees are there at church because someone they knew... first invited them. The bluegrass gospel jams provide that welcoming invitation atmosphere. Where else could my passion or your passion be so vividly displayed?

Change Of Heart

Before I started the Bluegrass Gospel Jams, I had a double bypass heart operation. When I awoke in the hospital, still alive, I made the decision to get more value out of my life. I searched and found principles that had everlasting peaceful impact. I asked myself the question, *"What do I enjoy doing?"* I made the appropriate decision to finish out my life doing the things I enjoyed. I found out that my perception of what was good for me was more important than money, job, and security. That's when I became a closer companion with God. I now get to share my faith with others by authoring books and promoting bluegrass gospel jam growth.

I had no money to start anything; nor did I have any premonition about what God could do through me. I simply started out on a faith journey that has blessed lots of people. Despite all the unexpected setbacks, I have persevered. My faith has grown and is still on the rise.

I have become a *"Scribe for God."*

I have become a catalyst for starting up bluegrass gospel jams.

I am the *"Great Encourager."*

I encourage you.

Please consider sending in your victory stories.

Sample Victory Story

Hi Ron,

This is Richard (and Eva) from Fort Morgan. Hope you are doing well and we want you to know that your health has been in our prayers. The Bluegrass Gospel Jams have been an answer to our prayers and I can't wait for your new E-Book to come out so I can get a copy.

Eva and I just want to say again how much we enjoyed our first Jam in Fort Collins and plan on attending as many Jams as possible in the future. In fact, I enjoyed it so much that I went out that following Monday and bought myself a new mandolin, which I also play fairly well. Now I can switch off between guitar, fiddle, and mandolin at future jams. That means I'm now interested in workshops for both fiddle and/or mandolin so you can put the word out for that. I am also willing to give workshops for beginning and intermediate bluegrass guitar, if anyone's interested. I've have given guitar lessons in the past and am able to teach anything except advanced bluegrass leads. I'll leave that to the Pros!

Eva and I plan to be at the opening of the Evans/Greeley Jam on March 3rd.

I have also met John Horner from the Sterling Jam and we will be participating in that event also. I already knew several members of his band "The Prairie Pickers" so I joined up and have started practicing with them.

This brings me to my last point, which was mentioned, in the latest Newsletter. Eva and I were planning on going to the Gospelgrass Festival in June anyway and I would like to help out with whatever you need. I have years of experience in operating sound equipment and am very good at it so I would like to volunteer for that position if it is still needed. This experience comes from more than 15 years as a semi-professional Country musician, band manager, and soundman. I have a fairly large sound system of my own as well as some nice recording equipment. Would you be interested in having your part of the festival recorded and edited to put on a CD or whatever? Just an idea. Anything else we can do to help just let me know.

Also I would like to know how does a band apply to perform at the Festival?????

Hope to hear from you soon and I guess I'll see you at the Evans/Greeley Jam on the 3rd.

Take care and God bless the good work you are doing.

Richard

Colossians 3: 17

And whatever you do, whether in word or deed, do it all in the name of the Lord Jesus, giving thanks to God the Father through him.

Ecclesiastes 2: 16

For the wise man, like the fool, will not be long remembered; in days to come both will be forgotten. Like the fool, the wise man too must die!

Proverbs 16: 3

Commit to the Lord whatever you do, and your plans will succeed.

Now What?

Become involved with Bluegrass Gospel Jams. Become a participator. Find a good location to start up a new Jam. Attend an existing Jam. Invite other friends and family to come. Learn to play an instrument. Attend an instrument workshop. Learn to sing. (Everyone can sing…if the group is big enough!) Learn how to *"put a song in your heart and a tap in your toe."*

You never know what kind of positive impact a gospel song can have on an audience. We have stories of how the Jams have changed lives. As one musician *"duo"* husband-and-wife alcoholic said, *"The Gospel Jam saved our lives."*

Please remember that God will help you whenever you give God control. God has helped me. I know he will do the same for you. *"Ask and you shall receive."*

Send in your victory stories as we grow the Bluegrass Gospel Jams together.

www.ingramcontent.com/pod-product-compliance
Lightning Source LLC
LaVergne TN
LVHW051832080426
835512LV00018B/2832